Migration and Poverty

Migration and Poverty

Toward Better Opportunities for the Poor

Edited by
Edmundo Murrugarra
Jennica Larrison
Marcin Sasin

THE WORLD BANK
Washington, D.C.

ISBN: 978-0-8213-8436-7
eISBN: 978-0-8213-8437-4
DOI: 10.1596/978-0-8213-8436-7

Library of Congress Cataloging-in-Publication Data
Migration and poverty : towards better opportunities for the poor / edited by Edmundo Murrugarra, Jennica Larrison, Marcin Sasin.
    p. cm.
  ISBN 978-0-8213-8436-7 — ISBN 978-0-8213-8437-4 (electronic)
1. Poverty—Developing countries—Case studies. 2. Developing countries—Emigration and immigration—Economic aspects—Case studies. 3. Developing countries—Emigration and immigration—Government policy. I. Murrugarra, Edmundo. II. Larrison, Jennica. III. Sasin, Marcin J. (Marcin Jan) IV. World Bank.
  HC59.72.P6M48 2010
  325.086'942—dc22

                                                                                    2010035683

Cover photo by Arne Hoel.

The data in all tables and figures in this book were compiled by the authors unless otherwise noted.

Contents

Conclusion   26
Annex   28
Notes   32
References   32

Chapter 3   **Work-Related Migration and Poverty**
                 Reduction in Nepal   **35**
                 Michael Lokshin, Mikhail Bontch-Osmolovski,
                 and Elena Glinskaya

                 Introduction   35
                 Data and Measures   37
                 Migration and Remittances in Nepal:
                     Descriptive Analysis   38
                 Work-Related Migration and Poverty:
                     Theoretical Considerations and
                     Empirical Specifications   44
                 Results   47
                 Conclusions   58
                 Annex   60
                 Notes   61
                 References   62

Chapter 4   **The Evolution of Albanian Migration and**
                 Its Role in Poverty Reduction   **67**
                 Carlo Azzarri, Gero Carletto, Benjamin Davis,
                 and Alberto Zezza

                 Introduction   67
                 International Migration Trends in the
                     Albanian Context   68
                 Remittances   77
                 Assessing the Impact of Migration
                     on Poverty   87
                 Conclusion   90
                 Annex   92
                 Variable Description   92
                 Notes   97
                 References   99

Figures

Tables

Foreword

Not often in the development profession does a new idea emerge that is able to capture the attention of scholars, policy makers, and development practitioners throughout the world—or bring fresh hope to a field in which many approaches have already failed to meet high expectations. International migration, however, still holds the promise of substantially accelerating development, poverty reduction, and the emancipation of people in general.

Indeed, there are more than 200 million migrants in the world now, and the money that migrant workers send home—over 300 billion dollars per year—dwarfs the amount of development aid and many other financial flows. This money bypasses the often wasteful bureaucracies and goes straight into the hands of families, where it is spent on necessities as well as on human and capital investment. For many countries migration has emerged as a common livelihood strategy, and remittances have become the largest source of foreign exchange.

Does migration help to reduce poverty—and if so, how and under what circumstances? These are important empirical questions to ponder if the world is to realize the full potential of migration. This book addresses these questions with recent research from the World Bank—including case studies from Albania, Nepal, Nicaragua and Tanzania—that illustrate the diversity of the migration experience and analyze the complicated nexus between migration and poverty reduction.

The research shows how migration expands the choices available to poor people and how it can contribute significantly to alleviating poverty. Unfortunately, migration opportunities are not equally distributed and vary depending on the level of skills and resources. So poor people tend to either migrate less or migrate to less lucrative destinations. And many countries may not be taking full advantage of the poverty-reducing potential of international migration.

One important message from the book is that reducing the costs of migration makes it more pro-poor. And although most of the policy levers to reduce the costs and release the benefits of migration are on the side of the industrialized countries, policy makers in the developing countries are not without the means to improve the situation and help their own migrants benefit more. The case studies offer a few examples of policies that can contribute to this objective.

It is our hope that this book will serve as a basis for further discussions on these important topics and that it will keep the theme of human mobility at the center of the development agenda.

Otaviano Canuto
Vice President
Poverty Reduction and Economic Management
World Bank

Acknowledgments

This book would not have been possible without the involvement of many people. First, the editors wish to thank the authors of the individual chapters and the case studies for their valuable contributions, their commitment to professional excellence, and their dedication to migration research, which no doubt stems from a firm belief that migration can bring a positive change to the lives of poor people.

Second, this book would not have been published had it not been for the continuous support and guidance of the management team of the World Bank's Poverty Reduction and Equity Group; in particular, Ana Revenga, Jaime Saavedra, Pierella Paci, and Louise Cord.

Christopher Humphrey helped make many of the chapters more readable, and Susan Graham and Stephen McGroarty from the World Bank Office of the Publisher carried the book very efficiently through the production process.

Last but not least, Nelly Obias and Jae Shin Yang provided extraordinary administrative assistance.

About the Editors and Contributors

Editors

Jennica Larrison: PhD Candidate and Assistant Teacher, The George Washington University, Trachtenberg School of Public Policy and Public Administration, Washington, DC.

Edmundo Murrugarra: Senior Economist, Social Protection Sector, Latin America and Caribbean Region, World Bank.

Marcin Sasin: Economist, Poverty Reduction and Equity Unit, Poverty Reduction and Economic Management Department, World Bank.

Contributors

Carlo Azzarri: Consultant, Poverty Reduction and Economic Management Sector, Africa Region, World Bank.

Kathleen Beegle: Senior Economist, Poverty and Inequality Unit, Development Research Group, World Bank.

Mikhail Bontch-Osmolovski: Consultant, Poverty and Inequality Group, Development Research Group, World Bank.

Gero Carletto: Senior Economist, Poverty and Inequality Group, Development Research Group, World Bank.

Benjamin Davis: Regional Social Policy Advisor, UNICEF Regional Office for Eastern and Southern Africa, Nairobi.

Stefan Dercon: Professor of Development Economics, Department of International Development, Oxford University.

Joachim De Weerdt: Research Director, Economic Development Initiatives Ltd., Bukoba, Tanzania.

John Gibson: Professor of Economics, Waikato Management School, Hamilton, New Zealand.

Elena Glinskaya: Country Sector Coordinator, Social Protection Sector, Europe and Central Asia Region, World Bank.

Catalina Herrera: Consultant, Inter-American Development Bank, Washington, DC.

Michael Lokshin: Lead Economist, Poverty and Inequality Group, Development Research Group, World Bank.

David McKenzie: Senior Economist, Finance and Private Sector Development Unit, Development Research Group, World Bank.

Alberto Zezza: Economist, Poverty and Inequality Group, Development Research Group, World Bank.

Abbreviations

ALSMS05   Albania Living Standards Measurement Survey 2005
FDI   foreign direct investment
FIML   full information maximum likelihood
GDP   gross domestic product
HBS   Household Budget Survey
IV   instrumental variable
KHDS   Kagera Health and Development Survey
LSMS   Living Standards Measurement Survey
NLSS   Nepal Living Standard Survey
OLS   ordinary least squares
PCA   principal component analysis
PPP   purchasing power parity
PSU   primary sampling unit
RSE   Recognised Seasonal Employer (New Zealand program)

CHAPTER 1

Overview

Introduction

This volume uses recent research from the World Bank to document and analyze the bidirectional relationship between poverty and migration in developing countries.[1] The case study chapters compiled in this book (from Tanzania, Nepal, Albania, and Nicaragua), as well as the last chapter on policy implications, illustrate the diversity of migration experience and describe the complicated nexus between migration and poverty reduction. Two main messages emerge from those studies:

- Evidence indicates that migration reduces poverty, but it also shows that the poor tend to either migrate less or migrate to low-return destinations. As a consequence, many developing countries are not maximizing the poverty-reducing potential of migration.
- The main reasons behind this outcome are difficulties in access to remunerative migration opportunities and the high costs associated with migrating. Research indicates that reducing migration costs makes migration more pro-poor. Hence, governments of developing countries should improve the poverty-reducing impact of migration. Several of the countries used as examples here have proposed policies toward this end.

The Poverty-Reducing Impact of Migration

The Promise of Migration to Reduce Poverty...

Migration has historically been a source of opportunities for people to improve their lives and those of their families. Today, the large differences in income between places—particularly countries—continue to motivate individuals to escape poverty through migration.

The potential advantages of migration for sending countries are numerous. Through remittances, migration provides a means of improving income and smoothing consumption; it enables households to overcome the lack of credit and cushion the risks involved in engaging in more productive activities; and migration can also act as a coping strategy in times of distress. Remittances can be spent on investments, such as housing and schooling, and directly on household consumption. Furthermore, new skills and education may be acquired at the place of destination and transferred back to the place of origin.

...Has Been Fulfilled

The case studies in this volume as well as other research provide evidence of the link between migration and poverty reduction.[2] For example, data show that almost 20 percent of the decline in poverty in Nepal between 1995 and 2004 can be attributed to increased work-related migration. Without migration, poverty in Nepal would have been more than 10 percent higher than it is now, while estimates for Nicaragua suggest that, without migration, the poverty rate would be 4 percentage points higher. Poverty rates for Tanzanians who stayed in their communities dropped by only 4 percentage points between 1991 and 2004, while it fell by 23 percentage points for those who moved out of their region. In Albania, regions that registered the highest reduction in poverty between 2002 and 2005 were those with the most increase in migration and remittances for the same period.

Evidence also points to the importance of migration as a coping mechanism for shocks, such as natural disasters or economic turbulence. During a drought, the likelihood of migration by the affected rural Nicaraguans to Costa Rica doubles. The two peaks of out-migration from Albania correspond to the aftermath of two severe economic shocks: the collapse of the command economy in the early 1990s and the collapse of the financial pyramid scheme in 1996.

This is not to discount the negative aspects of migration, which include family separation, potential exploitation of and various other risks to migrants, removal of entrepreneurial individuals from the community, and increased burdens on remaining household members. But with few exceptions, the evidence from this and other studies suggests that migrants and their families are better off compared to nonmigrants. Clemens and Pritchett (2008) estimate that, globally, three-quarters of the income difference between migrants and nonmigrants comes from migration itself. This leads them to the conclusion that since economic development is defined as an increase in human well-being, migration is not an alternative to economic development but rather economic development itself.

Despite the Benefits, the Poor Either Migrate Less Than Other Groups . . .

If migration brings such tangible benefits, the question then arises as to why more people do not escape poverty by migrating. Currently only 3 percent of the world's population live outside their country of birth. Moreover, it's usually not the very poor who migrate. The case studies of different countries in this volume as well as numerous other studies find a positive relationship between income status and likelihood of migration, with more migrants tending to come from the middle and upper end of the income distribution.[3]

One possible explanation for this is that the poor don't want to move. However, this hypothesis can be promptly rejected. Surveys show that many poor individuals in low-income countries express a desire to migrate, at least temporarily.[4] The disparity between the number of those eager to work abroad and the number actually doing so suggests that many poor people would like to escape poverty through international migration, but are not able to do so.

. . . Or Migrate to "Worse" Destinations

The poor who do migrate tend to move to places closer to their home that bring lower returns and may carry higher risks. This is understandable. If migration can be understood as the geographic allocation of labor resources to maximize income and reduce risk subject to a number of constraints, then the set of available migration opportunities will most likely differ between the poor and the better off. Migration choices will reflect not only household preferences among destinations but also the ability to actually "afford" those destinations.

Migration has costs, both economic and social, and requires would-be migrants to use resources that the poorest may not have access to. These resources include not only economic assets (income, savings, credit) but, of equal importance, human (entrepreneurship), social (networks), cultural (language), and political capital. The availability of these different factors determines the ability of the poor to migrate and, even more important, to choose certain migration destinations.

The case studies provide evidence for this hypothesis. Nicaraguan migrants to Costa Rica are poorer, less educated, and more likely to come from rural areas than those migrating to the United States. Clearly, moving to the United States implies a greater financial cost, requires social networks to enhance employment opportunities, and involves additional cultural barriers (for example, language). Migration to Costa Rica, on the other hand, is cheaper for Nicaraguans because of its proximity and cultural familiarity.

Similarly, only a very small percentage of Albanian migrants from poor, rural areas go to distant destinations. The majority move within Albania, while the remainder choose neighboring Greece, followed by Italy across the Adriatic. In Nepal, better-off international migrants tend to move to more lucrative Gulf countries, while the poorer migrants work mainly in neighboring India. Domestic migrants tend to come from the lower part of the income range.

Less profitable migration destinations can include other regions within a country as well as other developing countries—so-called South-South migration—two phenomena not nearly as well understood or researched as international migration to wealthy countries. Evidence in this volume and elsewhere suggests that domestic migration may be at least equally commonplace and relevant to understanding growth and poverty reduction patterns. For example, most Tanzanian migrants are domestic migrants, and many of them have successfully escaped poverty. In Nepal over the last decade, the elasticity of poverty reduction has been significantly higher for domestic as opposed to international migration.

Furthermore, statistics reveal that nearly one-half of migrants from developing countries move to other developing countries, and 80 percent of this movement takes place between neighboring countries.[5] Although these large labor flows come with relatively lower remittances, even these limited funds can have a significant poverty-reducing impact in the sending country. The importance of South-South migration also demonstrates that labor markets transcend national borders, and that regional labor markets may be appropriate units of analysis in contrast to the current tendency to consider only domestic labor market in isolation.

Consequently, the Poor Get Less and the "Better off" Get More out of Migration

Thus, more constrained households have access only to a set of "lower-quality" destinations, with lower returns (agricultural work) and higher risks (undocumented migration). These choices, in turn, may define the limits of the gains from migration, as the case studies suggest.

In Nicaragua, higher-income families are more likely to have a migrant in the United States, and gains associated with migrating to the United States are significantly higher than those from migration to Costa Rica. Albanian households with a migrant abroad are wealthier[6] and exhibit markedly different income and poverty dynamics. Households with migrants in neighboring Greece perceived that their situation got only somewhat better between 2002 and 2005, while the largest improvement happened for households with migrants to Italy and beyond.

In Nepal, individuals migrating to India—a "cheaper" destination compared to the Gulf countries—often earn only enough to survive and are rarely able to remit to their families at home. Likewise, in Tanzania, results showed that the farther one emigrates from the community of origin, the bigger are the gains.

Hence a Low Equilibrium Emerges: Poverty → Few or Low-quality Migration Opportunities → Less Poverty Reduction

A picture of a cyclical interconnection between poverty, remittances, and migration emerges in which migrants' socioeconomic status affects the quality of migration opportunities and destinations, which in turn affects the returns from migration and leads to different socioeconomic outcomes.

Accordingly, one of the main findings of this volume is that this self-sustaining cycle may make it difficult for the poor to lift themselves out of poverty through migration. In other words, the poverty reduction potential of migration is not fully utilized. The second finding is that because this underperformance is likely often caused by "market failures" such as imperfect information, lack of finance, and limited access on behalf of the poor, there is a rationale for instituting policies to improve this suboptimal equilibrium and increase the returns from migration for the poor.

Understanding the Constraints to Better Migration Outcomes for the Poor

The Poor Migrate Less Because of Lack of Opportunities and High Costs

Solid evidence indicates that the main barriers to greater migration and poverty reduction among the poor are few opportunities and high costs.

Migration opportunities and costs are, of course, in large measure a function of the policies of receiving countries, not of the sending countries. However, the policy section that follows offers an example of a program that has managed to open up new opportunities for international migration to some of the poor. This has been achieved through bilateral agreement between interested governments and the broad involvement of various actors.

But even when migration opportunities exist, the poor are usually the last to learn about them. A chapter in this volume finds, for example, that the first barrier to participation in a special migration program is lack of information: in both cases under study—Vanuatu and Tonga—less than a third of the target population had even heard of the program.

The issue of cost has many dimensions. Barriers related to geographic distance is one example of migration costs; it constrains access of people residing in less-connected (and usually poorer) areas to various avenues for migration. In Tanzania, those residing in better-connected districts are more likely to migrate. Nicaraguan households in regions close to Managua are more likely to migrate to the United States than those far away from the capital. In Albania, the poorer and isolated mountain region witnesses much less emigration.

Finance is another cost barrier. The poor often find it impossible to secure a loan to finance migration. Even if they do, loans come with exorbitant interest rates, such as the 30 percent real rate offered to the would-be migrants by Nepali moneylenders.

Some of the Barriers to Migration Are Imposed by Developing Countries Themselves

Many of the barriers and costs to emigration from developing countries are imposed on the poor by their own governments. One example is the time and monetary expense associated with obtaining a passport. Evidence in this volume demonstrates that a passport can cost over US$300, and in at least 14 countries a passport costs more than 10 percent of the average annual per capita income. Unsurprisingly, higher passport costs per capita are associated with lower migration rates. Lowering these costs by 1 percentage point is associated with a 0.75 percentage point increase in emigrants per capita. High passport prices are obviously more likely to be binding in the case of the poor would-be migrant.

In addition, a few countries raise more explicit barriers that affect the migration possibilities of certain groups, especially women, who face restrictions ranging from outright bans on travel to the need for permission of adult male relatives.

The Importance of Networks

One way households are able to increase returns and overcome the high costs of migration is through the use of migration networks. These networks consist of community, kinship, and friendship ties between migrants, return migrants, and nonmigrants.

Networks may provide migrants access to better jobs and significantly reduce uncertainty by providing loans to overcome financial constraints, assisting with housing and orientation post-arrival, lowering the costs of illegal border crossing, or managing the psychological impact of migration. It is the cost reduction aspect of networks that seems most important because, as discussed, the benefits are already such that many poor people want to migrate—they just can't overcome the barriers to doing so.

Accordingly, research commonly indicates that larger networks result in higher rates of migration. The Nepal case study shows that migration depends largely on the potential migrant's exposure to migration networks. Households in areas with a history of international migration are more likely to have an international migrant, while the likelihood of having a member migrate domestically is greater for households in regions with traditions of domestic migration. The experiences of Albania and Nicaragua also point to the importance of networks in migration.

Reduction in Costs Makes Migration More Pro-Poor

Evidence presented in this volume also suggests that reducing the costs of migration disproportionally benefits the poor. Migration networks can be used to demonstrate this link. (This is because networks reduce costs; hence, they can be used here as a proxy for migration costs.) It has been shown that the likelihood of a male head of household in Mexico migrating to the United States varies with the size of the migration network in his community: when the network is small, almost no males living in households below the US$1 per-person/per-day poverty line migrate, and migrants tend to be drawn from the upper-middle section of the expenditure distribution for a community. As the network grows, the likelihood of migration grows for all income groups, but more so for the poor. As a result, in communities where 20 percent or more of the community members have ever migrated, migration is heavily concentrated among those living on less than US$2 per person/per day, and the likelihood of migration is greatest for the very poor.

Similarly, the positive migration effect of social networks (and, by proxy, the positive effect of lower costs) appears to be more important for the less educated and poorer Nicaraguan would-be migrants. In Albania, increased emigration from the poor mountain region is reported to have resulted partially from growth of migration networks. As these networks grew, the education levels of migrants decreased, suggesting the inclusion of poorer, less educated candidates.

Hence, lowering the costs of migration allows the poor greater opportunity to participate in international migration, which they can use as a means of escaping poverty. This leads to the question of what policies governments can put in place to reduce costs, increase benefits, and facilitate the process of migration.

Policies to Increase the Returns from Migration for the Poor

This volume does not offer a comprehensive discussion of policies aimed at facilitating migration. One can find examples of such government policies in various developing countries. The Philippines is the best known, with a very proactive approach that includes licensing recruitment agencies, marketing its workers worldwide, and providing predeparture orientation seminars. However, in cases such as the Philippines, it is difficult to evaluate the impact of those policies on poverty levels, partly because of their systemic nature and partly because they have been in place for so long.

This volume also does not examine the immigration policies of rich countries. Clearly, such policies are extremely important in influencing not only the level of migration but also its characteristics, benefits, and risks. Such discussion is beyond the focus of this book, and also, the topic has been covered elsewhere (see Pritchett 2006).

Instead, the discussion in this volume is limited to a few examples of politically safe policies, such as lowering costs and expanding opportunities, that governments of developing countries can start pursuing today to increase the poverty-reducing impact of international migration. The main policies discussed are the following:

1. Reassessing the emigration framework and removing governments' barriers to emigration of their citizens, barriers such as high prices for passports and other restrictions.
2. Increasing the poverty-reducing benefits of remittances from present migrants by lowering remittance costs. Remittances are the most tangible benefits of migration and the most direct way of reducing poverty for the migrants' relatives remaining in the sending country. Lowering the costs of sending remittances has been the most discussed area of

intervention, partly because it is viewed as politically uncontroversial, and a variety of recommendations have been put forward in that regard.

3. Actively engaging in bilateral migration agreements to expand the opportunities for the poor to migrate. A new seasonal-worker program that takes workers from the Pacific Islands to New Zealand is one example.

Concluding Remarks

This volume argues that although migration increases income and often reduces poverty, the migration opportunities of the poor are different—among the poor there are fewer migrants, and they travel to "cheaper" destinations with lower returns. The main barriers to emigration encountered by the poor are lack of opportunities and high costs. This translates into lower returns and, very likely, less poverty reduction. As a result of this cyclical interconnection, the poverty-reducing potential that migration holds for developing countries is often not maximized.

An important finding is that reducing migration costs makes migration more pro-poor. As such, this volume argues that governments of developing countries have the means to expand opportunities and lower the costs of migration. Lowering barriers imposed by governments of sending countries and lowering remittance costs are examples of feasible policy changes to improve the poverty-reducing impact of migration.

By actively engaging in bilateral migration agreements, developed and developing countries can build the mutual trust necessary to increase the flow of unskilled people and enhance the pro-poor impact of migration programs by addressing the type of barriers that the poor are most likely to face, such as limited information and access to loans.

This does not mean, of course, that migration should be seen as the main driver of a country's development. Whether and under what conditions migration contributes to better (or worse) development outcomes for a country as a whole over the longer run is an active area of policy debate and research, and further investigation is necessary. The benefits depend to a great extent on the good policies of sending countries, which are beyond the scope of this study—for example, education provisions to facilitate better jobs for migrants and improve knowledge transfer, or a favorable financial sector and investment climate for increasing returns on remittances.

Notes

1. The book compiles research on international migration (the Nicaragua case study and the policy chapter), domestic migration (Tanzania), and both types of migration (Nepal and Albania).

2. See, for example, Adams and Page (2005); De Brauw, Taylor, and Rozelle (2001); de Haan (1999); Sabates-Wheeler, Sabatés, and Castaldo (2005); Skeldon (2003).

3. See, for example, Waddington and Sabates-Wheeler (2003).

4. See the last chapter, by Gibson and McKenzie, and those authors' own analysis from Intermedia/World Bank surveys from 2005–06; see also World Bank (2006).

5. See Ratha and Shaw (2007).

6. It should be noted that, in principle, the direction of causality between household wealth and migration is ambiguous. Migration could lead to greater wealth, greater wealth could improve an individual's ability to migrate, or other variables could influence both wealth and migration.

References

Adams, R. H., Jr., and J. Page. 2005. "Do International Migration and Remittances Reduce Poverty in Developing Countries?" *World Development* 33(10): 1645–69.

Clemens, M., and L. Pritchett. 2008. "Income per Natural: Measuring Development for People Rather Than Places." *Population and Development Review* 34(3): 395–434.

De Brauw, A., J. E. Taylor, and S. Rozelle. 2001. "Migration and Incomes in Source Communities: A New Economics of Migration Perspective from China." Department of Agriculture and Resource Economics, University of California, Davis.

de Haan, A. 1999. "Livelihoods and Poverty: The Role of Migration—A Critical Review of the Migration Literature." *Journal of Development Studies* 36(2): 1.

Pritchett, L. 2006. "Let Their People Come: Breaking the Gridlock on Global Labor Mobility." Center for Global Development, Washington, DC.

Ratha, D., and W. Shaw. 2007. "South to South Migration and Remittances." Working Paper, World Bank, Washington, DC.

Sabates-Wheeler, R., R. Sabatés, and A. Castaldo. 2005. "Tackling Poverty-Migration Linkages: Evidence from Ghana and Egypt." Working Paper. Development Research Centre on Migration, Globalisation and Poverty.

Skeldon, R. 2003. "Migration and Poverty." Johannesburg, South Africa.

Waddington, H., and R. Sabates-Wheeler. 2003. "How Does Poverty Affect Migration Choice? A Review of Literature." Working Paper T3, December 2003. Institute of Development Studies, Sussex.

World Bank. 2006. "World Development Report 2007: Development and the Next Generation." World Bank, Washington, DC.

CHAPTER 2

Patterns of Migration in Tanzania

Kathleen Beegle, Joachim De Weerdt, and Stefan Dercon

Introduction

Economic development is increasingly being linked with migration (see, for example, Clemens and Pritchett 2007; Vogler and Rotte 2000). Development may spur migration, and migration may result in more rapid economic growth. Standard economic theory offers multiple examples of how physical and economic mobility may go hand-in-hand. The Lewis model offers a stylized description of sectoral labor mobility, from agriculture into "modern" production processes, with increased earnings for migrants—initially well beyond the earnings for those who remain in agriculture and the village economy. The Harris-Todaro model emphasizes the migration process and that relative individual earnings incentives matter, so that both pull and push factors will drive migration. However, in equilibrium, migration would equalize expected returns, and no further migration would be observed; *on average*, welfare levels in rural and urban economies would equalize (Harris and Todaro 1970). Other work, such as the "new economics of migration" (Stark and Bloom 1985), emphasizes how migration is part of a more general livelihood strategy for the initial household as a whole, with migration as part of a welfare-maximizing strategy, with a clear role for overall household income growth as well as risk sharing. For example, Rosenzweig and Stark (1989) find that migration patterns for marriage in rural India are consistent with risk-sharing strategies of the initial household. Recent evidence has highlighted not only the role of networks in facilitating migration from home areas, but also how migration is closely linked to migrants' access to social networks in destination areas (Munshi 2003) or to community rates of out-migration (Kilic et al. 2007). Research by others, such as Hoff and Sen (2005), propose that kinship networks may establish barriers to emigration for members and prevent members from taking advantage of economic opportunities associated with migration.

While this emphasis on the process of migration in most recent empirical work has provided many insights, there are relatively few studies about this process from Africa. Moreover, studies on international migration outnumber those on domestic migration, while the data from this chapter suggest that the latter is more prominent and more relevant to understanding domestic growth patterns. This partly reflects the large data requirements for studying migration. As a temporal process, migration studies require either longitudinal data or detailed retrospective information. Panel data are increasingly being collected in developing countries to study the dynamics of household structure, demographics, and living standards, but the costs and difficulties of tracking people's movements mean that attrition may be relatively high. High attrition may also result in the loss of some of the most relevant households to a study of migration (Beegle 2000; Rosenzweig 2003).

Using data from a region in Tanzania, this chapter describes the characteristics of migration over a 13-year period. We focus on several aspects of migration: who migrates, why people move, household characteristics associated with individual moves, and, finally, the implications of this mobility on economic outcomes. Building on a detailed panel data survey conducted in 1991–94, we traced the sample of individuals in 2004. Detailed data on these individuals and their current households were collected at both baseline and in 2004, allowing for a thorough study of migrants' characteristics before their relocation and after, in their current living situation. The high recontact rates obtained make us well placed to study these issues.

We find that tracking individuals outside their baseline villages is crucially important for assessing welfare changes. The average consumption change of individuals found outside their baseline villages was more than 4 times higher than that of individuals found within the same village. Those who moved out of the Kagera region had nearly 10 times higher consumption change from 1991 to 2004, compared to those who remained in the community. These averages also translate into very different poverty dynamics patterns for the physically mobile and immobile. For those who stayed in the community, we see poverty rates drop by about 4 percentage points over 13 years.[1] For those who moved elsewhere within the region, we see poverty rates drop by about 12 percentage points; and for those who moved out of the region, poverty rates drop by 23 percentage points in the same period. For our whole sample of panel individuals, we find that average consumption between 1991 and 2004 increased by a bit more than US$60 per person per year, while the poverty rates fell by about 8 percentage points. Had we only focused on those individuals still residing in the baseline community, we would have concluded that average consumption rose by a bit under $30 and poverty rates declined by 4 percentage points. In other words, had we not interviewed people who moved out of the community—a practice found in many panel surveys—we would have seriously underestimated the extent to which poverty has decreased over the past 13 years in the Kagera region: we would have reported poverty reduction at about half of its true value. Aside from this, we would have omitted from our sample that part of the population with the highest information content on pathways out of poverty. Similarly, Clemens and Pritchett (2007) raise these issues in the context of income growth and international migration.

The Setting and Data

Between 1994 and 2004, Tanzania experienced a period of relatively rapid growth, using economic liberalization, a renewed trade orientation, a stable political context, and a relatively positive business climate to boost economic performance. Real GDP growth was of the order of 4 percent per year, while annual population growth was around 3.2 percent in the same period (URT 2004). However, this growth has not been sufficiently broad-based to result in rapid poverty reduction. On the basis of the available evidence, poverty rates have declined only slightly, and most of the poverty reduction progress has been made in urban areas. Nationally representative poverty data are available from the Household Budget Survey (HBS) for three points in time: 1991, 2000–01, and 2007 (NBS 2002; NBS 2009). Poverty rates declined over these three years from 39 percent, to over 36 percent, to 34 percent. However, poverty dropped only from 41 percent, to over 39 percent, to 38 percent in rural Tanzania, while it went from 28 percent, to over 18 percent, to 16 percent in Dar es Salaam.

These declines in poverty rates are not fast enough to attain the Millennium Development Goals.

The Kagera region is an area far from the capital and coast, bordering Lake Victoria, Rwanda, Burundi, and Uganda. It is overwhelmingly rural and primarily engaged in producing bananas and coffee in the north, and rain-fed annual crops (maize, sorghum, cotton) in the south. Relatively low-quality coffee exports and agricultural produce are its main source of income. It is not one the poorest areas of Tanzania, with mean per capita consumption near the mean of mainland Tanzania in 2000. Growth and poverty reduction appears to mirror the rest of Tanzania: real GDP growth was just over 4 percent per year between 1994 and 2004, but poverty is estimated to have fallen only by 2 percentage points (from 31 percent to 29 percent between 1991 and 2000–01, using the national data; see Demombynes and Hoogeveen 2007).

The challenge in Kagera may then seem to be rather representative for provincial Tanzania as a whole. While in some pockets, such as Dar es Salaam and other coastal areas, substantial growth and poverty reduction appears to have taken place, less-well-connected areas have not fared equally well. Kagera's challenge can be seen as reflecting the typical problems of land-locked, agriculture-based economies: how to deliver poverty reduction if the main engine of growth appears to be elsewhere (De Weerdt 2009). However, caution is necessary when using the existing evidence to fully assess the welfare changes linked to the recent decade of growth. Poverty reduction is about improved living standards of people, not regions, and as we will document below, people move to try to take advantage of and partake in changing circumstances. The data set used in this study can assess this appropriately.

The Kagera Health and Development Survey (KHDS) was originally conducted by the World Bank and Muhimbili University College of Health Sciences (MUCHS) and consisted of about 915 households interviewed up to four times from fall 1991 to January 1994 (at six- to seven-month intervals) (see World Bank 2004). The KHDS 1991 (first round) serves as the baseline data for this paper. Initially designed to assess the impact of the health crisis linked to the HIV-AIDS epidemic in the area, the survey used a stratified sample to ensure sufficient observations of families experiencing adult mortality. Comparisons with the 1991 HBS suggest that in terms of basic welfare and other indicators, it can be used as a representative sample for this period for Kagera.

The objective of the KHDS 2004 survey was to reinterview all individuals who were household members in any round of the KHDS 1991–94 survey and who were alive at the last interview (Beegle, De Weerdt, and Dercon 2006). This effectively meant turning the original household survey into an individual longitudinal survey. Figure 2A.1 in the Annex maps out how the 912 households from baseline split into the 2,719 households interviewed in the follow-up survey.

Although the KHDS is a panel of respondents and the concept of a "household" after 10–13 years is a vague notion, it is common in panel surveys to consider recontact rates in terms of households. Excluding households in which all previous members are deceased (17 households with 27 people), the field team recontacted 93 percent of the baseline households.[2] This is an excellent rate of recontact compared to panel surveys in both low-income countries and high-income countries. The KHDS panel has an attrition rate that is much lower than that of other well-known panel surveys summarized in Alderman et al. (2001), in which the rates ranged from 17.5 percent attrition per year to the lowest rate of 1.5 percent per year. Most of these surveys in Alderman et al. (2001) covered considerably shorter time periods (two to five years).

Much of the success in recontacting respondents was due to the effort to track people who had moved out of the baseline communities. One-half of the 2004 households were not in the baseline communities. Of those households tracked, only 38 percent were located near the baseline community. Overall, 32 percent of all households were not located in or relatively near the baseline communities. While tracking is costly, it is an important exercise, because, as will be shown below, it greatly improves recontact rates, and migrant households have quite different income dynamics.

Turning to recontact rates of the sample of over 6,000 respondents from baseline, Table 2A.1 shows the status of the respondents by age group (based on their age at first interview in the 1991–94 rounds). Older respondents were much more likely to be located if still alive, which is consistent with higher migration rates among the young adults in the sample. Excluding people who died, 82 percent of all respondents were reinterviewed. Table 2A.2 shows the location of respondents. Without tracking, reinterview rates of surviving respondents would have fallen from 82 percent to 52 percent (2,797 out of 5,394 survivors). Nonlocal migration is not trivial; restricting the tracking to nearby villages would have resulted in 63 percent recontact of survivors. Migration proved to be an important factor in determining whether someone was recontacted. While 8 percent of traced individuals resided outside Kagera, 43 percent of untraced individuals were reported to be residing outside the region.

Key Characteristics of Migration

Who Moves and Why

We divide the sample into three categories to examine the individual characteristics of movers and nonmovers. Specifically, for movers, the categories are those who moved to a nearby village (14 percent of the entire sample) and those who moved farther away (23 percent). The remaining 63 percent of individuals surveyed were residing in the same village in 2004 as in 1991. As shown in Table 2.1, not surprisingly, the most salient traits of movers are that they are younger on average and more likely to have never married. Women are more likely to move, as marriage (which is universal) is associated with relocating to the husband's community in this setting (patrilocality). Individuals who were the head, spouse of the head, or child of the head were less likely to move than others. Those residing in better-connected districts, such as Bukoba Rural and Bukoba Urban, were more likely to move.

Figure 2.1 plots the cumulative distribution function for consumption per capita for the three groups. At baseline, there was no difference in the poverty rate across groups (indicated by the intersection of the vertical

Table 2.1   Baseline Characteristics of Nonmovers and Movers

	Did not move	Moved to nearby village	Moved farther away
Age (years)	20.5	14.2	15.0
Male	0.53	0.34	0.45
Never married	0.32	0.65	0.62
Mother resides in household	0.50	0.50	0.44
Father resides in household	0.41	0.42	0.36
Head, spouse, or child of head	0.77	0.56	0.56
Education (years)	2.4	2.8	2.9
Completed primary	0.21	0.25	0.25
Chronic illness	0.15	0.07	0.10
Any children residing outside of household	0.75	0.21	0.26
District			
Biharamulo	0.08	0.07	0.09
Bukoba Urban	0.17	0.27	0.27
Bukoba Rural	0.31	0.30	0.35
Karagwe	0.15	0.15	0.08
Muleba	0.16	0.13	0.14
Ngara	0.12	0.09	0.07
Number of observations	2,797	626	1,971

Figure 2.1   Cumulative Density Function of Consumption per Capita in 1991 by Future Migration Status

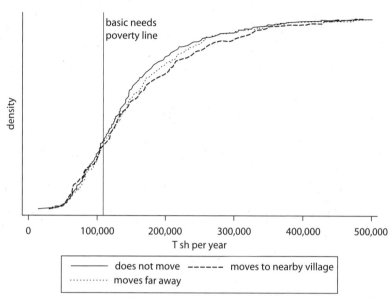

basic needs
poverty line

density

0   100,000   200,000   300,000   400,000   500,000

T sh per year

——— does not move   – – – – – – moves to nearby village
·············· moves far away

Note: The basic needs poverty line is 109,663 Tanzanian shillings (T sh) per year.

line in Figure 2.1 with the curves). Movers were slightly wealthier on average (indicated by the slight right shift in the curve for movers), although the differences in the means were not statistically significant.

Since many of the characteristics of migration are interrelated (such as age and never been married, or age and being household head), we examine the migration decision using multivariate analysis in Table 2A.3. Most of the patterns found in Table 2.1 remain in the multivariate results. The age-migration relationship is nonlinear. Age is associated with higher probability of moving for those under 20 in baseline; after that point, the age-migration relationship is negative. Males and not-yet-married persons are more likely to move. Persons residing with their mother or the head, spouse of the head, or child of the head are less likely to move than others. Education is positively associated with probability of migrating. As will be discussed below, the strong association of migration with individual traits, as opposed to the role of household characteristics, will be a critical aspect to the analysis of migration impacts on consumption growth. Specifically, the key variables for that work will be the relative position within one's household with respect to age, sex, and relationship to head, as well as interactions of these traits with other covariates.

Characteristics of Migration

Consistent with the demographic characteristics of movers, marriage was the most common self-reported reason for leaving the village (Table 2A.4). Over two-fifths of local migrants (41 percent) reported moving for marriage. Work-related motives were commonly reported for non-local moves, with reasons such as having found work, seeking work, and being posted to a job accounting for over 20 percent of these cases. Following parents was reported to have motivated 12 percent of such long-distance moves. In general, though, the reasons for moving are varied and often reflect sociocultural, economic, and life cycle–related motives.

In Table 2A.5, we show some of the basic characteristics of migrants' location as of 2004. Migrants may have moved to several places between 1991 and 2004, and we have only information to compare their 2004 location with the baseline location.[3] While migration is often associated with urbanization (or at least, not moving to more remote locations), we find that less than one-third of migrants are residing in less remote locations. Fully one-third actually reside in more remote areas of Tanzania, compared to their baseline location. Moves to less remote locations are associated with large average distances between origin and 2004 location, averaging 258 kilometers. This reflects the distance of Kagera from Dar es Salaam, the commercial capital on the opposite side of the country.

Household Splitting

An interesting phenomenon associated with individual migration is that the household as a unit splits up as members move out. Table 2A.6 describes the baseline characteristics of households for two groups of households, based on whether any member is located in another village or town by 2004. About 14 percent of households (122 out of 895) did not have any member locate to a new village or town. Migration is not a rare event for households in Kagera. For many traits, including male headship, age of head, education of head, wealth, and land holdings, there is no statistical difference between the two groups of households. However, households with higher education (measured by the highest level among members) and larger households are significantly more likely to have someone move.

Economic Impact of Migration

As noted above, migrants and nonmigrants did not have wealth or income differences at baseline. Yet when we examine their relative incomes in 2004 and relative income growth, a very different picture emerges.

Table 2.2 shows the poverty rate and consumption per capita for the sample for both years and the difference (growth). Among the entire sample, the poverty rate declined by 8 percentage points. This statistic, however, hides important differences between subgroups of the panel respondents based on their 2004 location. For those found residing in the baseline community, poverty rates dropped by 4 percentage points. Those who moved experienced larger declines with poverty rates dropping by 11, 13, and 23 percentage points for those who moved to neighboring communities, elsewhere in the Kagera region, and outside the region, respectively. A similar pattern can be noted with respect to average consumption per capita. While this grew by around US$65 for

Table 2.2 Average Consumption Movements of Panel Respondents, by 2004 Location

	Mean 1991	Mean 2004	Difference between means	N
Poverty headcount (%)				
Full sample	0.35	0.27	−0.08***	4,075
Within community	0.36	0.32	−0.04***	2,611
Nearby community	0.33	0.22	−0.11***	566
Elsewhere in Kagera	0.37	0.24	−0.13***	571
Out of Kagera	0.30	0.07	−0.23***	327
Consumption per capita (T sh)				
Full sample	159,217	225,099	65,882***	4,075
Within community	155,641	186,479	30,838***	2,611
Nearby community	166,565	230,807	64,242***	566
Elsewhere in Kagera	162,116	262,964	100,848***	571
Out of Kagera	169,994	457,475	287,480***	327
Food consumption per capita (T sh)				
Full sample	106,113	145,991	39,878***	4,075
Within community	103,889	121,919	18,030***	2,611
Nearby community	111,077	150,478	39,401***	566
Elsewhere in Kagera	108,323	168,022	59,699***	571
Out of Kagera	111,416	291,958	180,542***	327
Nonfood consumption per capita (T sh)				
Full sample	57,059	79,108	22,049***	4,075
Within community	55,383	64,560	9,177***	2,611
Nearby community	60,126	80,329	20,202***	566
Elsewhere in Kagera	58,450	94,942	36,493***	571
Out of Kagera	62,712	165,516	102,804***	327

Note: Significance of the difference with the 1991 value using a paired *t*-test: *** = 1%; T sh = Tanzanian shilling. Sample size is 4,075, including only observations for which all variables used in regressions analysis are available.

the whole sample, it grew by only $30 for those found in the same community and by $65, $100, and $287 for those who moved to neighboring communities, elsewhere in Kagera, and outside the region, respectively. Table 2.2 further shows that splitting the consumption aggregate up into its food and nonfood components gives the same picture. In other words, our entire basic assessment of welfare changes would have been wrong if we only had focused on those individuals still residing in the community, a practice found in many panel data surveys. We would have concluded that average consumption increased by only half of its true value, and poverty dropped by only half of its true value.

Figure 2.2 suggests that these conclusions are robust across the cumulative distribution of consumption. Panel a in Figure 2.2 depicts the cumulative density function for consumption per capita for those people who remained in the same community. Panels b and c show the same graph for respondents found residing in neighboring communities and elsewhere (in the Kagera region and outside the region). The poverty line is shown as a vertical line. As respondents were located farther from their baseline location, the difference between the 1991 and 2004 graphs becomes more pronounced. Note how, for people who remained in the baseline community, the 1991 and 2004 distributions lie close to each other under the poverty line and diverge above it, while for other mobility categories there is more divergence at the bottom of the graph. Thus in the baseline community very little movement out of poverty occurred, while those who moved out of the baseline community were more likely to improve their consumption—below or above the poverty line.

What drives the association between migrating and consumption growth?[4] Up to now, physical mobility per se has been used as a categorizing variable without regard to details on the destination to which people moved. By 1991, 68 percent of the sample were living in rural villages, of which a little over half were categorized by the survey team as poorly connected in terms of infrastructure. The rest of the sample were people living in (or close to) the regional capital, Bukoba (17 percent), or other small towns (14 percent). The income gains may be driven by moving to a better-connected center (for example, from a poorly connected to a better-connected village, or from a rural area to an urban center). About 10 percent of the sample moved to a better-connected area, and they experienced approximately 86 percent consumption growth. Those who moved to an equally connected area experienced consumption increases

Figure 2.2   Cumulative Density Function of Consumption per Capita

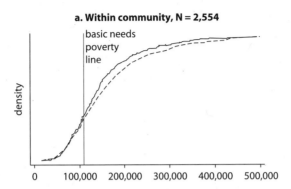

a. Within community, N = 2,554

b. Nearby community, N = 520

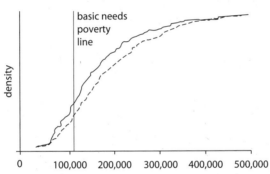

c. Elsewhere, N = 732

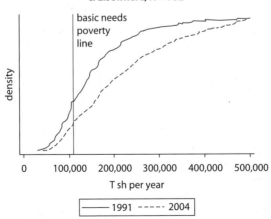

Note: The basic needs poverty line is 109,663 Tanzanian shillings (T sh) per year.

of 42 percent, while those who moved to a less-connected area experienced an increase in consumption of about 25 percent; this is still higher than the consumption growth of those who did not move. Clearly, it matters whether you move to a more or less remote area, but moving seems to matter in itself too.

A second plausible idea is that migration is capturing occupational or sectoral change. For example, consumption growth is highest for those who moved into nonagricultural activities (67 percent). Since migration may be tied to income, we explore this by looking at growth for the following groups: by sector change (stay in agriculture, move from agriculture to other occupations, stay in nonagricultural occupations, and move into agriculture from nonagricultural occupations) and by migration status. We find that irrespective of the sectoral change, migration is associated with higher average consumption. The only exception is for those who move into agriculture from nonagricultural activities, but this is a rare change.

Can we interpret these results as evidence that migration itself is a means of economic growth for individuals in Tanzania? That is a difficult question to address. Correlations between migration and income do not settle the issue of whether these changes are in fact directly related to migration or are spurious. A key problem is having access to data that allow a careful and convincing assessment of the relative welfare of migrants and nonmigrants, due to the standard evaluation problem that you cannot observe one person as both a migrant and a nonmigrant. A few studies have access to experimental data, such as international migration lotteries (for example, McKenzie, Gibson, and Stillman 2006), but most studies work with nonexperimental data. The key concern, that there is unobserved heterogeneity affecting both outcomes and the process of migration, bedevils most studies, usually leading to a quest for imaginative but convincing instruments for migration (see the review of the migration and poverty literature by McKenzie and Sasin 2007, and the references therein).

Although we do not have experimental data, we try to assess this through a number of empirical approaches. We use a difference-in-difference estimator, in which we compare consumption growth for those moving out of the initial community with that of those who stayed. As we have individual-level panel data, we can control for individual fixed heterogeneity affecting consumption levels. This resolves already a large number of possible sources of endogeneity usually mentioned as affecting studies of the impact of migration, such as risk aversion or ability, likely to affect both migration and income or consumption outcomes. However, it may be that certain families or individuals are likely to have higher *growth* in consumption due to factors that are also affecting the migration decisions. By looking within households, we can control for all initial household-level heterogeneity. This identifies the impact of migration using *within initial household* variation—differences between members of the same initial households, effectively controlling for initial growth paths. Furthermore, we can control for a wide set of individual level factors that may simultaneously affect consumption growth and migration.

It may be of concern that despite controlling for fixed individual heterogeneity and both fixed and time-varying household-level heterogeneity (including initial growth paths), unobserved individual factors may still affect migration as well as consumption growth, despite a broad set of observables used as controls. Finding plausible instruments that would satisfy exclusion from the consumption growth regression is not straightforward. We used three types of variables: migration pull factors, push factors, and variables reflecting social relationships. These instruments reflect the results of the previous section, that some of the migration decisions are related to relative individual traits within households rather than solely household-level factors.

In the initial household fixed effects regressions, we find a strong and significant effect of migration out of the community and a measure of the distance moved. Moving out of the community adds about 36 percentage points to the growth in consumption between 1991 and 2004. The regressions on distance moved suggest that the farther one moves, the greater the impact. As these regressions are identified using within initial household variation, these are very strong effects. Overall, migration has large impacts on consumption levels of migrants, but also causes strong divergence between people that initially lived together, including siblings and other family members. This does not preclude that substantial transfers take place between different split-offs, but definitely not enough to constitute within-household consumption smoothing. It provides little evidence for the theory that the migration decision is part of a household-level maximization strategy (although it cannot preclude it).[5]

We find (very remarkably) that the 2SLS (IV with fixed effects) results are identical to initial household fixed effects results. In other words, there is little or no evidence that unobserved individual time-varying heterogeneity affected the noninstrumented results. The conclusion is strong: being able to move out of the village or community appears to play a strong role in being able to experience larger consumption growth, and if those who moved had stayed behind, our evidence suggests that they would not have done as well. We perform a variety of checks to verify the robustness of these findings, which are described in detail in Beegle, De Weerdt, and Dercon (2008).

Taken together, this suggests that there are windows of opportunity—being in the right place at the right time—that certain categories of people can take advantage of: not having social and family constraints in a window of time when physical mobility has large payoffs. Missing these windows implies remaining trapped in a low-return environment.

Our results throw new light on the debate about the role of traditional values and norms in a modernizing society characterized by relatively high economic growth. People need to move to take advantage of opportunities that arise over time and space in the region, yet social norms can prevent some categories of people from moving. For example, Hoff and Sen (2005) theorize that kinship groups establish exit barriers for their members, because in some situations it can be in the interest of the kinship group to prevent some of its members from migrating. The analysis in Beegle, De Weerdt, and Dercon (2008) largely points to social and family norms interacting with pull (nearby towns) and push (shocks) factors as determinants of who can be allowed (or are chosen) to move. These are traits linked with age, gender, and social position in the household, as well as the interaction of these traits with distance to a town. People in their teens and twenties, with weaker ties to the households in which they live, unmarried individuals, and males have more freedom to take advantage of the windows of opportunity that come their way. Similarly, being head or spouse of the head will typically imply local responsibilities making it harder to leave.

This still raises the question of why more people do not move, and why these barriers remain in place if they are so welfare reducing.

Conclusion

Migration may be a pathway for economic development, but we often lack the longitudinal data required to study patterns of migration. This chapter uses unique panel data from Tanzania to explore the patterns of migration among Tanzanian households. Nearly half of all respondents migrated out of their baseline village or town between 1991 and 2004. Almost all of this is migration within Tanzania. Only about 14 percent of the baseline households had no household members residing outside the baseline village. Migration among members is the norm, rather than the exception. We find a number of individual traits associated with migration, whereas household characteristics are less likely to predict members moving out of the village. Moreover, consumption measured at baseline is not associated with future migration.

Individuals who migrate have higher consumption growth and higher rates of poverty reduction than nonmovers. Using a number of econometric techniques, we attempt to assess the causal impact of migration. We find that individuals who migrate do better, even when some migrate to more remote locations, and regardless of changes in their sector of work.

Annex

Figure 2A.1   KHDS 2004: Recontacting Respondents after 10+ Years

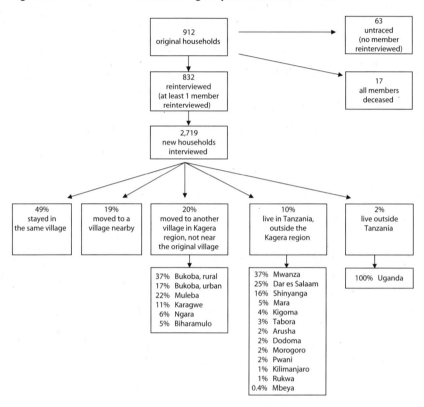

Note: KHDS = Kagera Health and Development Survey.

Table 2A.1   KHDS Individuals, by Age

	Recontacted		Deceased		Untraced		Reinterview rate among survivors (%)
<10 years	1,604		160		317		83.5
(Percentage)		(77.1%)		(7.7%)		(15.2%)	
10–19 years	1,406		104		412		77.3
(Percentage)		(73.2%)		(5.4%)		(21.4%)	
20–39 years	823		287		190		81.2
(Percentage)		(63.3%)		(22.1%)		(14.6%)	
40–59 years	436		148		34		92.8
(Percentage)		(70.6%)		(23.9%)		(5.5%)	
60+ years	163		262		9		94.8
(Percentage)		(37.6%)		(60.4%)		(2.1%)	
Overall	4,432		961		962		82.2
(Percentage)		(69.7%)		(15.1%)		(15.1%)	

Note: Sample of individuals ever interviewed in KHDS 1991–94 and alive at last interview. Age categories are based on age at first interview. KHDS = Kagera Health and Development Survey.

Table 2A.2   KHDS Reinterview Rates by Location

	Number	Location	Percent
Baseline sample	6,355		
Reinterviewed	4,432		
		Same community	63.1
		Nearby community	14.1
		Elsewhere in Kagera	14.4
		Other region	7.1
		Other country	1.3
Untraced	962		
		Kagera	56.7
		Dar es Salaam	12.3
		Mwanza	10.4
		Other region	7.9
		Other country	5.5
		Don't know	7.3
Deceased	961		

Note: Locations for untraced respondents were reported by other household members from the baseline survey who were successfully located, interviewed, and able to provide location information on the respondent. In some cases, this information comes from other relatives or neighbors residing in the baseline communities. KHDS = Kagera Health and Development Survey.

Table 2A.3   Probability of Migrating

	Moved out of village/town	Moved further away than nearby village
Age (years)	0.038***	0.030***
	(0.008)	(0.007)
Age squared	−0.001***	−0.001***
	(0.000)	(0.000)
Male	−0.398***	−0.193***
	(0.037)	(0.037)
Never married	0.778***	0.613***
	(0.089)	(0.088)
Mother resides in household	−0.154***	−0.182***
	(0.058)	(0.058)
Father resides in household	0.005	−0.082
	(0.066)	(0.069)
Head, spouse, or child of head	−0.428***	−0.242***
	(0.074)	(0.076)
Education (years)	0.034***	0.035***
	(0.010)	(0.010)
Chronic illness	−0.074	−0.000
	(0.067)	(0.065)
Any children residing outside of household	0.019	0.007
	(0.020)	(0.019)
Number of observations	5,390	5,390

Note: Probit estimation. District dummies also included. Significance level: *** = 1%.

Table 2A.4   Reasons for Moving

	Moved to nearby village	Moved farther than nearby village or outside region	All movers
Found work	2.7	5.8	3.5
To look for work	5.4	15.3	8.7
Posted on a job	1.2	1.6	1.0
Looking for land	7.1	6.1	8.7
Schooling	4.4	9.9	6.0
Marriage	41.1	22.8	28.9
Divorce	2.2	1.9	2.0
Parents died	4.7	3.1	3.7
To care for a sick person	0.5	0.6	0.7
To seek medical treatment	0.5	1.1	0.7
Following inheritance	5.1	2.8	5.8

(continued)

Table 2A.4   Reasons for Moving *(continued)*

	Moved to nearby village	*Moved farther than nearby village or outside region*	*All movers*
Other family problems	7.6	6.4	8.5
Follow parents	8.4	12.0	10.3
Follow spouse	0.5	0.8	0.8
Follow relatives	0.7	3.2	1.8
New house	1.2	0.0	1.4
Other	6.4	5.7	7.0
No reason reported	0.5	0.7	0.7
Total	626	1,012	1,638

Note: Reason for move pertains to the original move from the dwelling/compound at which the person was residing at baseline (and not necessarily the reason for choosing the current location as of the interview in 2004). Excludes movers who were not relocated in 2004.

Table 2A.5   Characteristics of Migration

Remoteness	*Percent of respondents*	*Average distance of move (km)*
Less remote location	28.9	258
Similar location	36.5	40
More remote location	34.6	39
Number of observations	1,633	

Note: Sample of respondents who located to a new village or region by 2004. Kilometers are calculated based on GPS location of village at baseline and location of household in 2004 interview. Remoteness is based on the changes in classification among six possibilities, in order of remoteness: island in Lake Victoria, remote village, connected village, urban center, district capital, regional capital.

Table 2A.6   Characteristics of Households by Future Migrant Status

	No members moved to another village by 2004	*Some members moved by 2004*
Male household head	0.78	0.73
Age of household head[a]	45.1	48.7
Years of education of head	4.0	4.2
Highest years of education among members[a]	5.6	6.4
Water from river/stream/other	0.71	0.73
Toilet facility	0.91	0.92
Good flooring[a]	0.09	0.18
Value of physical stock (T sh)	2,058,241	2,198,099
	[1,185,393]	[1,448,865]

(continued)

Table 2A.6   Characteristics of Households by Future Migrant Status *(continued)*

	No members moved to another village by 2004	Some members moved by 2004
Value of durable goods (T sh)	57,700	79,444
	[0]	[0]
Land value (T sh)	1,279,800	1,139,444
	[876,722]	[777,293]
Acres of land owned	4.2	4.1
Consumption per capita (T sh)	227,030	196,580
Household size[a]	3.98	6.17
Number of observations	122	773

a. Indicates that the difference between columns is statistically significant at 10%. Median values in brackets.
T sh = Tanzanian shilling.

Notes

1. Defined as the proportion of population below the "basic needs" poverty line of T sh 109,663 per year.
2. Throughout this discussion and the calculations of migration rates, individuals who were deceased by 2004 are not included.
3. Likewise, the reason for migrating reflects the reason they left the village and, for multiple moves, it is not necessarily the reason they are living in the current location. Similarly, nonmigrants may have relocated between 1991 and 2004, but at some point they returned to the baseline village/town where they were residing during the 2004 survey.
4. The rest of this section draws heavily on Beegle, De Weerdt, and Dercon (2008), where a more in-depth discussion and full results are presented.
5. We have data on transfers sent by different split-off households to each other, and there is little evidence that such transfers are, on average, of the order of magnitude that could offset the consumption differences.

References

Alderman, Harold, Jere R. Behrman, Hans-Peter Kohler, John Maluccio, and Susan Cotts Watkins. 2001. "Attrition in Longitudinal Household Survey Data: Some Tests for Three Developing-Country Samples." *Demographic Research* 5(4): 79–124.

Beegle, Kathleen. 2000. "Economic Mobility in Indonesia and Vietnam: What Missing Data Can't Tell Us." RAND, Santa Monica, CA.

Beegle, Kathleen, Joachim De Weerdt, and Stefan Dercon. 2006. "Kagera Health and Development Survey (KHDS), 2004: Basic Information Document." http://go.worldbank.org/793WPKOR00.

————. 2008. "Migration and Economic Mobility in Tanzania: Evidence from a Tracking Survey." Policy Research Working Paper 4798. World Bank, Washington, DC.

Clemens, Michael, and Lant Pritchett. 2007. "Is Migration Development? Global Estimates of Income per Natural." Draft. Center for Global Development, Washington, DC.

De Weerdt, Joachim. 2009. "Defying Destiny and Moving out of Poverty: Evidence from a 10-Year Panel with Linked Qualitative Data from Kagera, Tanzania." EDI, Tanzania. http://www.edi-africa.com/research/joachim.

Demombynes, Gabriel, and Johannes Hoogeveen. 2007. "Growth, Inequality and Simulated Poverty Paths for Tanzania, 1992–2002." *Journal of African Economies* 16(4): 596–628.

Harris, John, and Michael Todaro. 1970. "Migration, Unemployment and Development: A Two-Sector Analysis." *American Economic Review* 60(1): 126–42.

Hoff, Karla, and Arjit Sen. 2005. "The Kin System as a Poverty Trap?" Policy Research Working Paper 3575. World Bank, Washington, DC.

Kilic, Talip, Gero Carletto, Benjamin Davis, and Alberto Zezza. 2007. "Investing Back Home: Return Migration and Business Ownership in Albania." Policy Research Working Paper 4366. World Bank, Washington, DC.

McKenzie, David, John Gibson, and Steven Stillman. 2006. "How Important Is Selection? Experimental v. Non-Experimental Measures of the Income Gains from Migration." IZA Discussion Paper No. 2087. Policy Research Working Paper 3906. World Bank, Washington, DC.

McKenzie, David, and Marcin J. Sasin. 2007. "Migration, Remittances and Human Capital: Conceptual and Empirical Challenges." Policy Research Working Paper 4272. World Bank, Washington, DC.

Munshi, Kaivan. 2003. "Networks in the Modern Economy: Mexican Migrants in the United States Labor Market." *Quarterly Journal of Economics* 118(2): 549–97.

NBS (National Bureau of Statistics Tanzania). 2002. "Household Budget Survey 2000/01."

————. 2009. "Household Budget Survey 2007 Analytical Report." http://www.nbs.go.tz/HBS/Main_Report2007.htm.

Rosenzweig, Mark. 2003. "Payoffs from Panels in Low-Income Countries: Economic Development and Economic Mobility." *American Economic Review* 93(2): 112–17.

Rosenzweig, Mark, and Oded Stark. 1989. "Consumption Smoothing, Migration, and Marriage: Evidence from Rural India." *Journal of Political Economy* 97(4): 905–26.

Stark, Oded, and David Bloom. 1985. "The New Economics of Labor Migration." *American Economic Review* 75(2): 173–78.

URT (United Republic of Tanzania). 2004. "The Economic Report, 2004." President's Office, Planning and Privitisations.

Vogler, Michael, and Ralph Rotte. 2000. "The Effects of Development on Migration: Theoretical Issues and New Empirical Evidence." *Journal of Population Economics* 13(3): 1432–75.

World Bank. 2004. "User's Guide to the Kagera Health and Development Survey Datasets." http://go.worldbank.org/793WPKOR00.

CHAPTER 3

Work-Related Migration and Poverty Reduction in Nepal

Michael Lokshin, Mikhail Bontch-Osmolovski, and Elena Glinskaya

Introduction

With an average per capita GDP of about $240 ($1,420 in purchasing power parity), Nepal is the poorest country of South Asia. About 42 percent of the Nepali population lived on income below the poverty line in 1995–96, 46 percent of the adult population remained illiterate in 2003 (Central Bureau of Statistics 2003), and almost half the children five years and under were malnourished (Nepal Ministry of Health 2002). During the period of stabilization and liberalization in the mid-1980s and early 1990s, the Nepali economy grew at about 5 percent per year. The impact of these relatively high rates of economic growth on improvements in living standards was dampened by the country's high population and urban-centered growth, limited access to basic services, poor governance, and increasing political instability. Economic growth slowed in the early 2000s due to a global economic slowdown, diminishing export markets, and the escalation of violence resulting in declaration of a state of emergency.

Despite these negative trends, the overall poverty rate in Nepal declined to about 30 percent by the end of 2003. Between 1995 and

2004, real per capita expenditures grew by more than 40 percent in real terms (World Bank 2006). That growth in per capita expenditure was accompanied by increasing income inequality, as indicated by the Gini coefficient, which climbed from 0.34 in 1995 to 0.44 in 2004.

The common explanation for these developments, both in the press and among local and international scholars, is the sharp increase in remittances from Nepali expatriates working abroad. Indeed, more than a million prime-age (mostly male) adults are currently working outside Nepal. Remittances from expatriates grew at 30 percent per year, and from less than 3 percent of GDP in 1995 to about 15 percent by the end of 2003 (World Bank 2004), exceeding the combined share of tourism, foreign aid, and exports. According to official government statistics, about 1 billion U.S. dollar comes into the country as formal remittances, and inflows through private and unofficial channels could be even larger (Thieme 2003). The growing numbers of migrants who secure work and send remittances back home have a profound effect on socioeconomic, demographic, and political issues in Nepal.

Remittances affect economy-wide resource allocation. At the macro level, inflation, exchange, and interest rates are determined by the amount of money coming into the country in the form of remittances (for example, Djajic 1986). At the household level, remittances provide a means of achieving consumption smoothing (Yang and Choi 2005) and mutual insurance (Stark and Lucas 1988), as well as alleviating liquidity constraints (Taylor et. al 2003). Household decisions about the labor market activities of household members, investments in human and physical capital, fertility, and migration also depend on the amount of remittances the household receives (Docquier and Rapoport 1998).

A macro-level study of 74 low- and middle-income countries by Adams and Page (2005) finds that remittances have strong poverty-reducing impact. Adams (1989, 1991) presents micro-evidence on the importance of remittances for poverty reduction in rural Egypt, while Adams (2005) summarizes the results of micro-level analysis in several countries, finding that poverty reduction in Bangladesh, Ghana, and Uganda could be attributed to the effects of remittances. Gustafsson and Makonnen (1993) report that removing remittances in Lesotho would raise the poverty rate from 52 to 63 percent, and Barham and Boucher (1998), in examining the net effects of migration and remittances on income distribution in Nicaragua, find that migration and remittances increase average household income and income inequality when compared with the no-migration counterfactuals. Du, Park, and Wang (2005) studied the effects of migration and remittances on poverty in China, finding that without migration and remittances, the aggregate poverty rate would increase from 14.4 to 15.4 percent. Other recent papers by McKenzie and Rapoport (2005) and McKenzie, Gibson, and Stillman (2006) estimate the overall impact of remittances on income distribution in Mexico, taking into account their direct and indirect effects on receiving households and the spillover effects on neighboring communities.[i]

The goal of this chapter is to provide empirical evidence of the effect of differential migration strategies on poverty in Nepal. We model the effect of remittances and work migration on consumption of households with a migrant. Using the cross-sectional sample of the nationally representative Nepal Living Standard Survey of 2004, we estimate a model of household migration decisions jointly with the consumption equations by the method of full information maximum likelihood (FIML) with instrumental variables. The method takes into account unobserved household characteristics that could simultaneously affect household migration decisions and household income. We simulate counterfactual expenditure distributions to determine the effect of work-related migration on the levels of aggregate poverty and inequality in Nepal. While most of the recent papers on the effect of migration on inequality and poverty have controlled for heterogeneity and selection in terms of unobserved characteristics, to the best of our knowledge this is the first study using FIML to estimate the trivariate selection model in this context. The novelty of the study resides on separating different effects of domestic and international migration on household welfare.

Data and Measures

Our analysis is based on the data from the second (2004) round of the Nepal Living Standard Survey (NLSS). We also use the data from the first (1996) round of the NLSS and Nepal Census of 2001 for descriptive results, and to construct the aggregate lagged data at the ward and district levels. The NLSS is a nationally representative survey of households and communities conducted between June 1995 and June 1996 (NLSS-I) and April 2003 and April 2004 (NLSS-II) by the Nepal Central Bureau of Statistics. The survey's instruments gather detailed information about the household demographic composition, the labor status of the household members, their health and educational achievements, and various sources of household income, including income in-kind, individual wages, and remittance and transfers received in the year preceding the survey (Central Bureau of Statistics 2006).

We use per capita consumption expenditure as an indicator of household welfare. Our consumption aggregate includes monthly household expenditures on food and nonfood items, imputed housing expenditures, and a stream of services from durables, as well as cash expenditures and imputed expenditures for home-produced goods. To assure comparability across the regions, all monetary indicators are deflated to 2004 national average prices. The poverty line for the analysis is constructed using cost-of-basic-needs approach (World Bank 2006). The cost of the poverty basket in 2004 all-Nepal prices equals Nr 7,694 per year per person—equivalent to US$107 or US$590 in purchasing power parity (PPP).

A serious limitation of our data is that households with migrants are identified only if they reported remittances in the previous year. Three groups of households could be misclassified under this definition. The first group consists of households with migrants who send no remittances. The second group comprises households that receive remittances but do not report them. Finally, some households could receive remittances from individuals who are not household members. Classifying these households as having no migrants would bias estimates of the impact of migration on household consumption. Although the direction of the bias is unclear a priori, the size of the bias is proportional to the sizes of these three groups. Lokshin and Glinskaya (2008) compare the proportion of migrants in the total population from the 2001 Nepal Census with the proportion of households with remittances in the NLSS data, and conclude that the bias resulting from misclassified households would most likely also be small.

Migration and Remittances in Nepal: Descriptive Analysis

The history of foreign employment in Nepal dates back almost 200 years, when Britain began recruiting men, known as Gorkhas, from the hillsides of Nepal into the British armed forces. After India's independence in 1947, the Indian military also began enlisting Nepali men. Currently, about 3,500 Nepali solders serve in the British army, and more than 50,000 Nepalese are enlisted in the Indian military. India was the first country to attract civilian migrants from Nepal. The inflow of working migrants to India has increased sharply since the 1950s (Sheddon 2005).[1]

The Foreign Employment Act of 1985 was the first legislative document to officially recognize the benefits of international migration (Jha 1999). Around that time, foreign labor migration from Nepal extended from India to the countries of the Southeast and Far East, and later to Arab Gulf States. The total number of Nepali migrants working abroad reached 750,000 in 1997, contributing about Nr 35 billion to the country's economy in the form of remittances (Sheddon, Adhikari, and Gurung 2000). The reform of the administrative system during 2000 and 2001 resulted in a boost in both domestic and international migration. Before the reforms, passports could only be obtained in the country's capital, but under the new regulations, district offices were given the authority to issue passports and other travel documents (World Bank 2006).

Domestic migration has increased in Nepal since the success of government's efforts to control endemic malaria in the Terai in the early 1950s. Interdistrict migration constitutes 13.2 percent of domestic migration (Central Bureau of Statistics 2003), while rural–urban migration represents 25.5 percent, and rural-to-rural migration is significantly higher at 68.2 percent. The poor rural regions of the mid- and far-west underwent a net out-migration, with migrants moving from the mountainous and hillside areas to the Terai and urban areas.

The NLSS is the first data source to provide statistically accurate estimates of levels of and trends in work-related migration from Nepal, and on the amount of money sent home in remittances. According to NLSS, 23 percent of households in Nepal received remittances in 1995, and that proportion climbed to about 32 percent in 2004. Further, the share of households with remittances from abroad grew from 10 to 17 percent between the survey's two rounds. The average amount of remittances increased from about Nr 22,000 (in 2004 prices) or 36 percent of mean household yearly consumption expenditure in 1995, to Nr 35,000 or 44 percent of mean expenditure in 2004.

In 2004, household size was an important determinant as to whether a household received international remittances. Figure 3.1 shows the increase in incidence and the amount of remittances by household size for 1995 and 2004. Focusing first on the top panels of the graph, the proportion of households receiving remittances grows monotonically with household size in both years. The incidence of remittances increased more rapidly with household size in 2004 compared to 1995. For example, in 1995 there is virtually no difference in the proportion of remittance recipients among households with three to eight members. In 2004 only about 10 percent of households with two or three members received

Figure 3.1   Incidence of Migration and Amount of Remittances by the Household Size

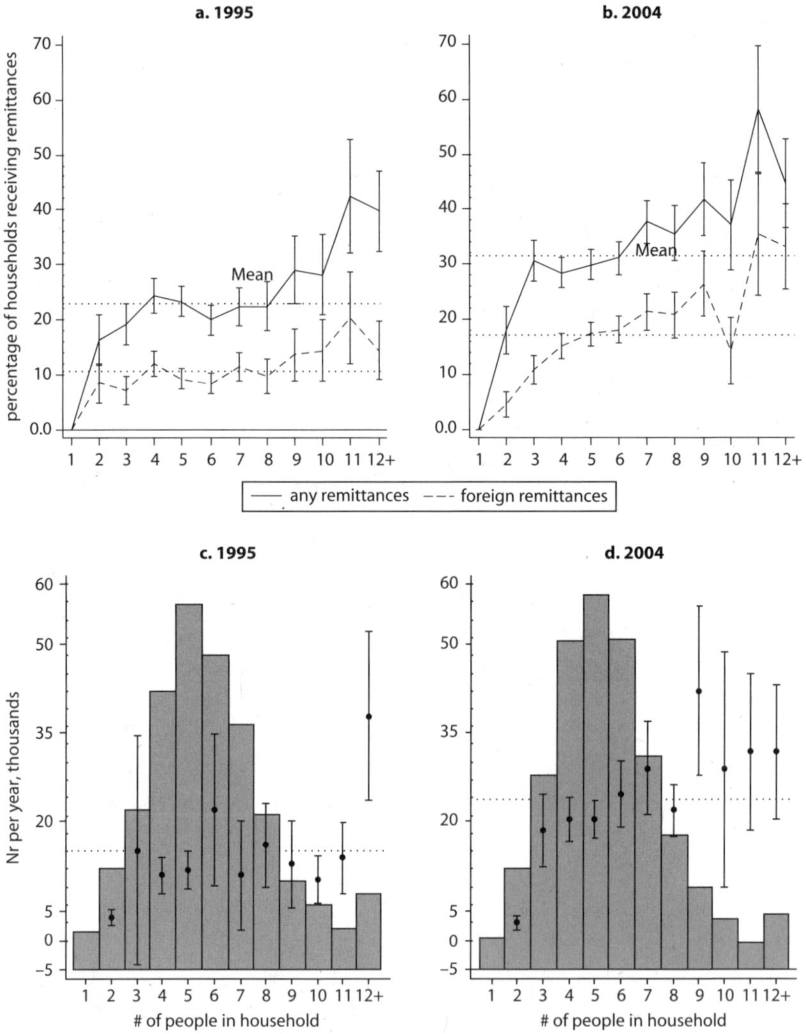

Source: Nepal Living Standard Survey (NLSS) 1995, 2004.
Note: Whiskers indicate 95 percent confidence Intervals for the means. The histogram of the household size distribution is shown in gray in parts c and d. Nr = Nepalese rupees.

money from abroad, while that proportion is more than twice as high for households with eight or more members. The changes in the amounts of remittances by household size are shown on the lower panel of the graph. The plot indicates that in 1995 households with different sizes received almost the same amount of money, while the 2004 data show that the amount of remittances increased with household size.

The overall increase between 1995 and 2004 in the proportion of households with remittances can almost entirely be attributed to the growth of remittances from abroad. The incidence of remittances is higher in rural than in urban Nepal. The proportion of households receiving remittances from within the country increased only marginally between 1995 and 2004, and even declined in Katmandu (top section of Table 3.1). The share of households receiving money from abroad increased uniformly across the country.

Looking at the proportions of households receiving remittances by caste (bottom part of Table 3.1), Dalit households have the highest probability of receiving money from outside Nepal (25 percent), while the incidence of external remittances is much lower among Newars and Terai Janjatis. At the same time, only 10 percent of Dalit households receive remittances from Nepal. This might suggest that poor job opportunities at home prompt Dalit households to concentrate their job search efforts abroad.

Poorer households tend to receive remittances more frequently than better-off households; however the amount of remittances received is significantly less for poorer households compared to their better-off counterparts. The original socioeconomic status of the household may therefore predetermine the level of remittances received. The correlations between household income and the incidence and amount of remittances are shown in Figure 3.2. The main difficulty in illustrating this relationship is that current income is endogenous to the remittances. We attempt to address this problem by constructing a two-year-lagged asset index to proxy for pre-migration income.[2] Overall, the incidence of remittances (or migration) is higher among (asset) poor households. It reaches 35 percent for the poorest households in Nepal, and declines monotonically to about 10 percent for the richest households. The correlation between the amount of remittances and household wealth goes in the opposite direction. Households with the highest lagged asset index receive significantly larger amounts of money from working migrants than poor households. Thus, poorer households receive lower remittances from their migrating household member than better-off households.

Individual profiles constructed using NLSS data reveal that almost all international migrants are male (97 percent), aged 15 to 44 years, and either sons or husbands of the person receiving remittances. Brothers represent about 10 percent of the total number of donors. In 1995, 92 percent of Nepali migrants worked in India, and the rest were spread among Malaysia (6 percent); Bhutan; and Hong Kong SAR, China (Table 3.2). As of 2004, international migrants were living in 10 countries: 69 percent

Table 3.1 Percent of Households Receiving Remittances by Region of Nepal

	Receive remittances from Nepal		Receive remittances from abroad		Receive any remittances		Group proportions	
	1995–96	2003–04	1995–96	2003–04	1995–96	2003–04	1995–96	2003–04
Region								
Katmandu	14.2	7.7	3.6	5.6	17.8	13.3	2.9	5.8
Other urban areas	13.0	16.9	6.3	14.1	19.2	31.0	4.4	10.6
Rural West mount/hills	10.6	11.0	19.6	29.6	30.2	40.6	26.3	21.7
Rural Eastern mount/hills	11.2	17.0	2.0	9.1	13.2	26.1	23.6	21.2
Rural western Terai	12.0	12.5	10.6	19.2	22.6	31.7	13.9	13.5
Rural eastern Terai	14.7	14.5	11.0	18	25.7	32.5	28.8	27.2
Caste								
Brahman\Chhetri	13.4	15.8	11.0	19.9	24.4	35.7	37.4	31.0
Dalit	11.9	9.8	15.3	25	27.2	34.8	8.3	8.0
Newar	13.1	14.5	3.6	7.7	16.7	22.2	5.8	7.7
Terai-Hill Janajatis	10.0	14.5	9.6	15.2	19.6	29.7	24.4	26.9
Muslim\Other minorities	13.0	12.1	11.4	18.2	24.4	30.3	24.1	26.4
Land holdings a year ago								
No farm plot	11.4	14.1	11.1	13.3	22.6	27.4	28.3	23.2
Farm plot <0.5 ha	13.1	13.6	11.9	18.7	25.1	32.3	33.1	37.9
Farm plot 0.5–1 ha	12.6	12.6	10.4	19.1	23.0	31.7	17.3	20.9
Farm plot: 1–2 ha	12.4	14.5	10.2	20.0	22.6	34.5	13.4	12.4
Farm plot >2 ha	11.2	17.8	5.2	18.0	16.5	35.8	7.9	5.7
Lagged durable asset index								
No assets	11.1	14	11.5	18.2	22.7	32.2	61.6	42.0
Asset poor (1st–33rd percentile)	11.1	15.3	10.1	17.1	21.2	32.4	16.1	21.9
(33rd–66th percentile)	14.5	14.3	10.4	18.0	24.9	32.3	14.5	20.6
Asset rich (66th–100th percentile)	20.4	11.1	5.5	16.5	25.9	27.6	7.8	15.6
Total	12.3	13.9	10.7	17.7	23.0	31.5	100	100

Figure 3.2   Non-Parametric Regression of the Incidence of Migration and Amount of Remittances by Lagged Asset Index

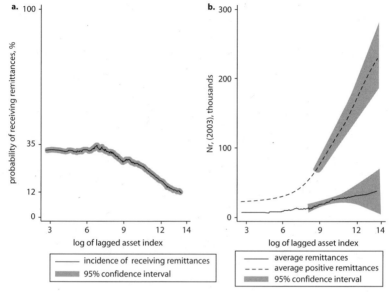

Source: Nepal Living Standard Survey (NLSS) 2004.
Note: Nr = Nepalese rupees.

Table 3.2   Percent of Migrants by Country of Destination, NLSS 1995 and 2004

	1995			2004		
	All migrants	International migrants	International, excluding India	All migrants	International migrants	International, excluding India
Nepal	58.88			48.09		
India	37.86	92.08		35.57	68.52	
Saudi Arabia				5.87	11.31	35.93
Malaysia	2.53	6.14	77.54	3.36	6.47	20.57
Qatar				2.6	5.01	15.92
United Arab Emirates				0.97	1.87	5.93
United Kingdom				0.78	1.5	4.77
United States				0.62	1.2	3.82
Hong Kong SAR, China	0.33	0.79	10.03	0.44	0.86	2.72
Japan				0.3	0.58	1.84
Other	0.4	0.98	12.43	1.39	2.67	8.49
Total	100	100	100	100	100	100

Note: NLSS = Nepal Living Standard Survey.

worked in India, 18 percent in Arab countries, and the rest worked in the United Kingdom; Japan; Hong Kong SAR, China; and the United States. Remittances from abroad constituted 76 percent of the total remittances in 2004. The largest share of international remittances came from Saudi Arabia, Qatar, and the United Arab Emirates (35 percent), followed by 30 percent from India, 17 percent from other Asian countries, and the remainder from United Kingdom, United States, and other countries.

Work-Related Migration and Poverty: Theoretical Considerations and Empirical Specifications

Remittances sent home are the most tangible benefit of work-related migration for Nepali households. On the production side, remittances enable households to overcome the constraints of credit and risk of engaging in modern and more productive activities (Stark 1991). Remittances can be spent on housing and schooling, and directly on household consumption. But remittances are only one of the consequences of migration. When a young, able, and productive male household member leaves home, multiple adjustments need to be made among those left behind. Migration changes the relative productivity of the remaining household members; affects household preferences in terms of risk aversion and uncertainty; and provides new information—for example, on new technology, type of crops, and so on. Women who previously worked in the labor market may find it optimal to stop working and devote all their time to home production (Nandini 1999). Agricultural households might decide to augment their income with off-farm activities. Migration also has implications for the health and educational attainment of the migrant's children (Hilderbrandt and McKenzie 2004; McKenzie and Rapoport 2005). The observed consumption behavior and poverty status of households receiving remittances are determined by the cumulative effects of these changes.

In this analysis we model how the observed income distribution compares to the counterfactual distribution without migration and remittances. Our theoretical framework relies on several assumptions. First, we assume that households have a choice to send a migrant to work within Nepal or abroad. This assumption imposes certain restrictions on the sample for empirical estimations. We also assume that migration has to be planned ahead. Before the migration takes place, multiple arrangements need to be made. If traveling abroad, a Nepali migrant has to apply for and obtain a visa, get an international passport, and purchase a ticket.

Additionally, a migrant's household incurs expenses in the form of migration broker fees and traveling costs (Bhattrai 2005). This preparation process could take several years depending on the country of destination. The time and the costs of internal or seasonal migration to India might not be as high, but we can still assume that certain expenses have to be incurred in order to send a migrant to work.

Consider a simple two-period model of household utility maximization. In time period 1, a household decides that one of its members will migrate. This involves three possible alternatives: migration abroad, migration within Nepal, and no migration. Each state has an associated cost for a household. Such costs could, in case of migration, include transportation costs, visa and document processing fees, money to cover initial expenses, and so forth. To decide whether to embark on migration or not, a household compares its expected net benefits in each state (in period 2) and selects the state with the highest utility payoff. Households observe the realized labor market outcomes in time period 2: once settled in the new location, migrants inform households about their wages and local market conditions become known. With this information, households make decisions about member participation and market work hours and investment, adjusting their consumption level accordingly (for details of the model see the Annex).

Identification Strategy: Migration and Consumption Decisions
Our theoretical model guides an identification strategy for the empirical estimation. The model separates migration and consumption decisions in time, which allows us to assume that certain factors (variables) affecting the migration decision in time period 1 have no direct impact on household consumption in period 2.

The first instrument, the proportion of migrants in a ward in 2001, is constructed based on the 2001 Nepal Census (Central Bureau of Statistics 2003). That proportion could be interpreted as a proxy for the extent of village-level migration networks. We argue that household consumption in 2004 should not be directly affected by the migration networks in 2001. Carringon, Detragiache, and Vishwanath (1996) and Munshi (2003) test the role of networks in promoting migration, and find a greater propensity toward migration in villages with existing migrants—meaning that there is propensity for new migrants to follow in the footsteps of existing migrants. When in the host country, Nepali migrants develop extensive social networks that link them with their relatives and friends at home (Yamanaka 2000). Such networks lower the costs of migration for villagers by providing information about job opportunities outside Nepal, helping potential migrants secure employment, supplying credit to cover reallocation expenses, and ameliorating housing costs upon arrival. Relying on a similar identification strategy, Woodruff and Zenteno (2001) and McKenzie and Rapoport (2005) analyze the effects of migration on children's health and schooling outcomes in Mexico; Du, Park, and Wang (2005) study the relationship between migration and rural poverty in China; and Taylor and Mora (2006) investigate the effect of migration on expenditure patterns of rural households in Mexico. We expect this instrument to affect the probability of international migration and have small or no influence on the probability of migration within Nepal.

To construct an instrument for domestic migration, we use data from the first round of the NLSS. The variable for this instrument is the proportion of domestic migrants in a district in 1995. The underlying rationale is similar to the one discussed above, and we expect this instrument to have a positive and significant effect on the probability of domestic migration.

Our identification strategy requires that lagged migrant networks influence household consumption only through current migration. The presence of ward or district characteristics or shocks that simultaneously influence migration and household consumption would violate our identification restrictions. For example, better road infrastructure in a ward, or its proximity to a large urban center, could reduce the costs of migration and, at the same time, affect a household's returns on productive activities by providing better access to markets. We endeavor to control for time-persistent unobserved factors by including a set of ward-level characteristics in our empirical specification. These variables can capture many unobserved factors affecting both the household's migration decision and its current consumption level. Nevertheless, we cannot completely rule out the presence of latent local characteristics that are correlated with our instruments and simultaneously affect household consumption behavior. Lokshin and Glinskaya (2008) show that in the presence of unobservable time-variant characteristics, our results would provide lower bounds for the true effect of work-related migration on household consumption.

The identification strategy relies on the assumption that households' migration and consumption decisions can be separated. In the model, households first decide about the work-related migration of its members, and then about the household consumption. In the alternative framework of life-cycle maximization with perfect foresight and endogenous migration decision (Mesnard 2004), the exclusion restrictions for the instruments would not be valid. We argue, however, that the sequential model of household decision making better describes the behavior of households in the highly uncertain political and economic environment of Nepal.

Explanatory Variables and the Sample for Estimations

The predictions of the theoretical model determine the choice of our explanatory variables. These variables could be grouped conceptually into two categories. The first group describes factors affecting household production. These include the household demographics, education of female household members, and variables describing ethnicity. We also include variables on a lagged land ownership and lagged asset index as proxies for household wealth. The lagged asset index was constructed based on the estimated value of the flow of services provided by the durable goods. In our calculation, we include durables purchased by households at least two years prior the date of the survey (2001 and older). We then classify all households according to their wealth status, based on the percentiles of their lagged asset index. Our specification also contains a variable on amount of pensions received over the past year. The second group of variables comprises characteristics related to the region and ward.

Results

Migrating, within or outside Nepal, is largely dependent on the exposure to migration networks, household characteristics, and household location (see Table 3.3 for the estimation results of the migration choice model). Households in areas where international migration has a history of occurring are more likely to have an international migrant household member, while the likelihood of having a household member migrating domestically is greater for households in wards with domestic migration traditions. Large households and households with large female and elderly populations are more likely to have migrant members. Furthermore, residents outside of the capital, Katmandu, are more likely to migrate than those residing in Katmandu.

Factors that aid in determining destination choice include household wealth, and ward literacy and employment characteristics. International migrants are from both wealthy and poor households, while domestic migrants are typically from poorer households. High proportions of illiter-

Table 3.3   FIML Estimation of the Migration Choice Part of the System (1–3)

	Domestic migration		International migration	
Base category: No migration	Coefficient	Std. error	Coefficient	Std. error
Share of domestic migrants in district, 1995	1.059***	0.343	−0.418	0.423
Share of international migrants in a ward, 2001	0.165	0.250	1.267***	0.268
Household demographics (before migration)				
Household size	0.158***	0.017	0.127***	0.017
Share of children 0–3: Omitted variable				
Share of children 4–7	−0.192	0.364	0.162	0.318
Share of children 8–15	−0.058	0.276	−0.416	0.260
Share of men 16–64	1.156***	0.352	0.236	0.347
Share of women 16–64	1.996***	0.299	1.312***	0.306
Share of elderly	2.952***	0.355	0.932**	0.368
Number of married couples	−0.379***	0.056	−0.089*	0.049
Maximum education of women in the household	0.005	0.027	0.024	0.027
Ethnicity: Reference category: Brahman \ Chhetri				
Dalit	−0.268**	0.120	0.021	0.114
Newar	−0.244*	0.133	−0.452***	0.141
Terai-Hill Janajatis	−0.161**	0.072	−0.107	0.087
Muslim \ Other minorities	−0.281***	0.098	−0.103	0.095
Land holdings a year ago: Reference category: No farm plot				
Farm plot <0.5 ha	−0.061	0.076	0.037	0.079
Farm plot 0.5–1 ha	−0.247**	0.103	−0.100	0.098
Farm plot: 1–2 ha	−0.144	0.113	−0.029	0.111
Farm plot >2 ha	−0.156	0.137	−0.192	0.143
Lagged durable asset index: Reference category: No durables				
Asset poor (1st–33rd percentile)	0.057	0.069	−0.135**	0.068
(33rd–66th percentile)	−0.056	0.073	−0.141*	0.076
Asset rich (66th–100th percentile)	−0.324***	0.097	−0.139	0.091
Total pensions per capita	−0.015	0.013	0.016**	0.008
Geography dummies: Reference category: Katmandu				
Other urban areas	0.702***	0.167	0.565***	0.165
Rural west mount/hills	0.563**	0.229	1.042***	0.239
Rural eastern mount/hills	0.574***	0.198	0.479**	0.210
Rural western Terai	0.655***	0.225	0.739***	0.229
Rural eastern Terai	0.807***	0.196	0.838***	0.201
Log of distance to market center	−0.041	0.031	−0.015	0.029

(continued)

Table 3.3   FIML Estimation of the Migration Choice Part of the System (1–3) *(continued)*

	Domestic migration		International migration	
Base category: No migration	Coefficient	Std. error	Coefficient	Std. error
Ward level variables				
% illiterate, among age 15+	−0.544	0.396	0.029	0.422
% literate or 1–4 years of education	−0.556	0.594	0.416	0.536
% completed 5–7 years of education	−0.197	0.610	0.405	0.577
% employed in wage job	−0.053	0.391	0.481	0.451
% self-employed	0.549**	0.250	−0.031	0.332
Log of average household expenditure, 1995	0.063	0.135	0.131	0.139
Gini coefficient, 1995	0.022	0.584	−0.914	0.622
Casualties from conflict, district level	−0.024	0.060	−0.036	0.056
Constant	−3.170**	1.325	−3.553***	1.345
Number of observations	3620			
Log-likelihood	−4,264.00			

Note: FIML = full information maximum likelihood. Significance level: * = 10%, ** = 5%, *** = 1%. Standard errors are adjusted for clustering on a ward level.

acy in a ward preclude domestic migration, while self-employment creates a greater probability of domestic migration.[3]

Proximity to others who migrate provides knowledge about the migration process, destination opportunities, and logistics, creating a greater probability of migration for the exposed. Focusing first on the results for the choices of migration states, households living in wards with a historically higher proportion of international migrants are significantly more likely to migrate abroad compared with households without migrants. Households residing in districts with larger shares of domestic migrants are more likely to send their members to work in locations within Nepal. This relationship is consistent with the predictions of our theoretical model and indicates that our instruments have a significant effect on the households' choice of migration status, while emphasizing the importance of migration networks.[4]

The probability of migrating depends upon household characteristics. Large households and households with a higher proportion of adult women and the elderly are more likely to have a migrant. Compared with Brahman and Chhetri, other castes are less likely to migrate within Nepal, and the Newars prefer not to migrate abroad. Land ownership does not affect the probability or destination of work-related migration, whether locally or abroad. A paper by Lokshin and Glinskaya highlights that the decision of a male member to migrate is determined, particularly in the rural areas of Nepal, by the changes in productivity of the household members left behind. In a simple model developed in the paper, a husband and a wife contribute to the home production. If the husband's inputs in home production are complimentary to the wife's inputs, the husband's migration would decrease the wife's productivity at home. If inputs of spouses are substitutes, the husband's migration would increase the wife's productivity at home. The paper argues that for households with larger land holdings, the productivity of household members left behind is more likely to decline because of migration. This "pull" factor would prevent male members of households with large land plots from migrating. At the same time, such households are usually better off and less constrained in terms of resources necessary for migration.

The probability of a household having a domestic migrant is higher among poorer households compared with wealthier households (based on the percentiles of the lagged asset index). At the same time, individuals from the extremes of the wealth distribution are more likely to work abroad. We might speculate that the members of the wealthy households tend to migrate to Gulf States, while the poorest migrants mainly work in India.

Individuals residing in Katmandu are less likely to migrate compared with those living in other areas of Nepal. This could be attributed to better labor market conditions in the country's capital.[5] The probability of international migration is higher among households from the rural western mountains and hills (see Figure 3.3). Households in wards with a higher proportion of illiterate residents are less likely to have a member migrate to locations within Nepal.

Overall, the observed household characteristics, in particular geographical and ward characteristics, play a more important role in determining the level of consumption in households without migrants compared with those with a migrant. Table 3.4 illustrates the results of the FIML estimation of consumption equations for the three states of migration. While a household's human and productive capital has a strong effect on consumption in households without migrants, these factors become less important for households with a migrant when remittances contribute a significant share to the household budget. By comparing the estimation results of a three-choice model with the results of a model where international and domestic migration destinations are combined into one category, the log-likelihood test rejects the equality of

Figure 3.3   Percent of Households with Work-Related Migrants, by Region

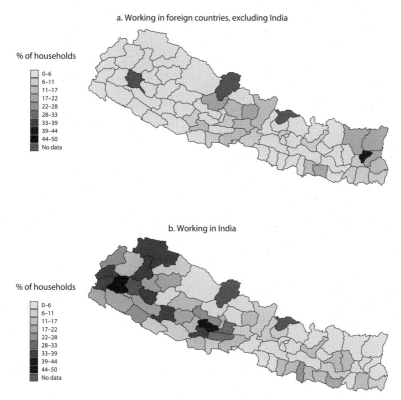

a. Working in foreign countries, excluding India

% of households

- 0–6
- 6–11
- 11–17
- 17–22
- 22–28
- 28–33
- 33–39
- 39–44
- 44–50
- No data

b. Working in India

% of households

- 0–6
- 6–11
- 11–17
- 17–22
- 22–28
- 28–33
- 33–39
- 39–44
- 44–50
- No data

the coefficients in the consumption regressions for international and domestic migrants. This justifies the assumptions of our theoretical model about the differences in returns on productive and human capital characteristics between international and domestic migrants.

The demographic composition and particularly the dependency ratio have a significant impact on per capita consumption expenditure. Households with larger shares of children aged 0 to 3 years have lower per capita consumption relative to other households. Households with better-educated female members have higher per capita consumption levels. The size of landholdings has a positive and significant impact on household consumption regardless of migration status. For households with international migrants, those possessing more than two hectares of land have significantly higher per capita consumption compared with landless households. Households from the upper percentiles of the lagged

Table 3.4 FIML Estimation of Expenditure Equations of the System (1–3)

	Domestic migration		International migration		No migration	
	Coefficient	Std. error	Coefficient	Std. error	Coefficient	Std. error
Household demographics (before migration)						
Household size	-0.120***	0.015	-0.101***	0.028	-0.074***	0.008
Share of children 0–3: Omitted variable						
Share of children 4–7	0.319*	0.189	0.137	0.147	0.175	0.109
Share of children 8–15	0.278*	0.144	0.613***	0.133	0.359***	0.072
Share of men 16–64	0.161	0.182	0.386	0.256	0.228**	0.103
Share of women 16–64	0.272*	0.154	0.493	0.344	0.747***	0.105
Share of elderly	-0.180	0.184	0.222	0.377	0.260*	0.148
Number of married couples	0.150***	0.044	0.081*	0.046	0.067***	0.018
Maximum education of women	0.034**	0.017	0.081***	0.015	0.086***	0.007
Ethnicity: Reference category: Brahman \ Chhetri						
Dalit	-0.151*	0.086	-0.233***	0.065	-0.170***	0.038
Newar	0.049	0.070	0.074	0.120	-0.002	0.029
Terai-Hill Janajatis	-0.075	0.054	-0.125***	0.047	-0.217***	0.026
Muslim \ Other Minorities	0.024	0.068	-0.151**	0.064	-0.132***	0.031
Land holdings a year ago: Reference Category: No farm plot						
Farm plot <0.5 ha	-0.003	0.053	0.007	0.053	0.062**	0.024
Farm plot 0.5–1 ha	0.215***	0.065	0.055	0.065	0.143***	0.030
Farm plot: 1–2 ha	0.181***	0.069	0.120*	0.067	0.206***	0.031
Farm plot >2 ha	0.266***	0.086	0.320***	0.070	0.330***	0.041

Lagged durable asset index: Reference category: No durables

Asset poor (1–33rd percentile)	0.053	0.049	0.070	0.055	0.004	0.020
(33rd–66th percentile)	0.175***	0.051	0.185***	0.054	0.167***	0.022
Asset rich (66th–100th percentile)	0.558***	0.064	0.518***	0.079	0.491***	0.028
Total pensions per capita	0.019**	0.007	0.022***	0.005	0.015***	0.003
Geography dummies: Reference category: Katmandu						
Other urban areas	-0.103	0.104	-0.044	0.193	0.195***	0.047
Rural west mount/hills	-0.063	0.134	-0.284	0.270	0.241***	0.075
Rural eastern mount/hills	-0.102	0.126	-0.225	0.175	0.114**	0.054
Rural western Terai	0.039	0.134	-0.199	0.212	0.218***	0.060
Rural eastern Terai	-0.071	0.133	0.003	0.218	0.299***	0.059
Log of distance to market center	-0.024	0.022	-0.017	0.017	-0.023**	0.010
Ward level variables						
% illiterate, among age 15+	-0.250	0.225	-0.239	0.220	-0.369***	0.116
% literate or 1–4 years of education	0.029	0.314	-0.354	0.448	-0.115	0.182
% completed 5–7 years of education	0.516	0.392	-0.329	0.380	-0.603***	0.200
% employed in wage job	0.099	0.330	-0.080	0.213	-0.117	0.147
% self employed	-0.333**	0.154	-0.144	0.143	-0.223**	0.093
Log of average hh expenditure, 1995	0.148*	0.076	0.261***	0.077	0.320***	0.041
Gini coefficient, 1995	0.340	0.287	0.212	0.345	0.052	0.212
Casualties from conflict, district level	0.081**	0.039	0.027	0.034	-0.010	0.021
Constant	-0.504	0.743	-1.757	1.181	-2.782***	0.390
Number of observations	3,620					
Log-likelihood	-4,264.00					

Note: Significance level: * = 10%; ** = 5%; *** = 1%. Standard errors are adjusted for clustering on a ward level.

asset index and households receiving pensions have higher per capita expenditure regardless of migration status.

Our estimations also demonstrate strong regional variation in the level of household consumption for households without migrants: households residing in Katmandu have lower levels of consumption expenditures compared with households from other regions of Nepal. For households with international and domestic migrants, the regional effects are less pronounced. Certain local conditions seem to be significantly correlated with levels of household well-being. For example, households in wards with a high incidence of illiteracy are significantly poorer compared to households in wards with a better-educated population. Households either without migrants or with domestic migrants residing in wards with larger shares of self-employment are comparatively worse off.

Migration and Poverty Reduction

Over the last decade, elasticity of poverty reduction in Nepal is significantly higher for domestic migration than international migration. Using the estimated parameters of the system of equations, we simulate the effect of migration and remittances on distribution of per capita consumption given: (1) no migration, (2) migration in 2004 at 1995 levels, (3) 10 percent growth in domestic migration, and (4) 10 percent growth in international migration. When predicting household expenditures in a counterfactual state with no migration, we use information on the number of distinct senders of remittances and their age and gender to adjust the household size for the presence of would-be migrants, as well as all variables constructed using the household size and shares of various age-gender groups.

We construct four counterfactual scenarios (Table 3.5). The first column of Table 3.5 shows the actual rates of poverty, mean expenditure, and inequality for households exhibiting the three different states of migration. In 2004, 29.9 percent of the Nepali population had per capita consumption below the poverty line; average per capita consumption was Nr 14,930 per year, and the Gini inequality reached 0.409.

In the scenario of no migration (the second column in Table 3.5), households with migrants have the same returns on their observed characteristics as households without migrants: the size of the migrant households is increased by the number of migrants, and remittances are set to zero. Our simulations show that without migration the poverty rate in Nepal would have increased from the current 30.0 to 33.6 percent. The share of the poor among households with domestic migrants would have

Table 3.5   Simulated Levels of Expenditure, Poverty, and Inequality Rates for Different Migration Scenarios

Migration scenarios	Actual	No migration	Level of migration as of 1995/96	+10% point increase in domestic migration	+10% point increase in international migration
Household types			Poverty rate (%)		
All Households	30.0	33.6*	31.8*	27.6**	29.5
Households with no migrants	30.6	30.6	30.6	27.6**	29.3
Households with migrants within Nepal	22.9	46.3**	30.0**	22.9	25.5
Households with migrants abroad	32.8	34.9	37.2	30.7	32.8
			Average expenditure, Nr thousands		
All Households	1.493	1.405*	1.446*	1.561*	1.515
Households with no migrants	1.493	1.493	1.493	1.585*	1.536
Households with migrants within Nepal	1.576	1.087**	1.401**	1.576	1.527
Households with migrants abroad	1.441	1.341	1.328	1.478	1.441
			Inequality rate (Gini)		
All Households	0.409	0.405	0.407	0.412	0.412

Note: Shaded cells indicate that the poverty rates and average expenditure of these households are not affected by the simulated policy changes. Nr = Nepalese rupees. Significance level: * =10%; ** = 5%. The significance tests are calculated taking into account clustering at a ward level.

risen to about 46 percent (from 23 percent), and for households with international migrants, poverty would have increased to 35 percent (from 33 percent). Inequality would remain virtually unchanged. The consumption expenditure of households without migrants would remain unaffected, while the average consumption of households with domestic or international migrants would fall.

In the second scenario, the values of our two instruments are adjusted such that the proportions of domestic and international migrants are the same in 2004 as they were in 1995. This simulation results in higher overall poverty (a change from 30.0 to 31.8 percent), and higher poverty rates both among households with domestic migrants (a change from 22.9 to 30.0 percent) and among those with international migrants (32.8 to 37.2

percent). Inequality would decline. We can decompose the change in poverty between 1995 and 2004 into components that represent the contributions of the changes in domestic and international migration (nonmigrant households sending a migrant) to the total poverty change and the interaction component. This decomposition demonstrates that the growth in international migration between 1995 and 2004 decreased total poverty by 1.2 percentage points, while the growth in internal migration and the interaction component are responsible for a 0.6 percentage point reduction in poverty in Nepal.

The last two columns of Table 3.5 present the results of simulations for the hypothetical scenarios of a 10 percentage point growth in the levels of domestic and international migration. These simulations are based on implicit assumptions that this growth is caused by a decrease in the cost of migration and that the average amount of remittances a migrant sends home remains constant. Poverty in Nepal would be reduced by 2.4 percentage points if domestic migration were 10 percent higher, and poverty would decline by 0.5 percentage points if international migration were 10 percentage points higher. Both scenarios lead to rising inequality.

The important conclusion that emerges from these simulations is that the elasticity of poverty reduction in Nepal over the past decade is significantly higher for domestic migration than it is for international migration. One explanation for the different effects of domestic and international migration could be that remittances derived from work in foreign countries are more likely to be invested in productive assets and real estate. This is often attributed to the notion that households receiving international remittances tend to treat such funds as positive transitory income shocks that should be invested. Local remittances are treated as a mixture of transitory and permanent income and are more often used for consumption (Alderman 1996; Yang and Choi 2005).

In attempts to disentangle heterogeneity in the impact of migration and remittances on poverty, we simulate poverty rates for different types of households (Table 3.6). Households with a migrant living in other urban areas of Nepal and in rural western Terai experienced the most significant boost in consumption. Dalit households appear to gain less from sending their members to work in other regions of Nepal or abroad. Relative to the counterfactual scenario of no migration, landless (probably urban) households or those owning large land plots seem to benefit more from migration.

With an estimated increase in poverty of 3.6 percentage points, based on the counterfactual of no migration, the impact of changes in migration

Table 3.6   Simulated Changes in Predicted per Capita Consumption for Different Counterfactual Scenarios by Household Characteristics
Nr ten thousands

			Expected consumption		
Conditional on:	Actual	No migration	Level of migration as of 1995/96	+10% point increase in domestic migration	+10% point increase in international migration
Ethnicity					
Brahman/Chhetri	1.850	1.752	1.796	1.934	1.872
Dalit	1.052	1.033	1.030	1.088	1.059
Newar	2.670	2.557	2.611	2.770	2.696
Terai-Hill Janajatis	1.174	1.068	1.123	1.232	1.205
Muslim \ Other minorities	1.254	1.182	1.213	1.316	1.269
Land holdings a year ago					
Landless households	1.862	1.737	1.804	1.937	1.891
Farm plot <1 ha	1.296	1.224	1.255	1.362	1.314
Farm plot 1–2 ha	1.549	1.465	1.501	1.619	1.571
Farm plot >2 ha	1.876	1.762	1.810	1.943	1.912
Lagged durable asset index					
No Assets	1.021	0.963	0.989	1.068	1.035
Asset poor (1st–33rd percentile)	1.076	0.988	1.035	1.142	1.093
(33rd–66th percentile)	1.471	1.380	1.422	1.550	1.491
Asset rich (66th–100th percentile)	3.104	2.949	3.015	3.210	3.157
Geography dummies					
Katmandu	3.495	3.334	3.418	3.591	3.541
Other urban areas	2.476	2.291	2.391	2.572	2.527
Rural western mount/hills	1.187	1.154	1.157	1.241	1.203
Rural eastern mount/hills	1.137	1.064	1.105	1.196	1.150
Rural western Terai	1.269	1.177	1.223	1.368	1.280
Rural eastern Terai	1.388	1.300	1.336	1.443	1.414
Total	1.493	1.405	1.446	1.561	1.515

for work (together with associated remittances) in Nepal is somewhat lower than the impacts for other countries, even though most of these studies estimate the impact of remittances only. Adams (2005) attributes the effect of remittances to 5 percentage points of poverty reduction in Ghana, 6 percentage points in Bangladesh, and 11 percentage points in Uganda. Completely removing remittances would raise poverty rates by 8 percent points in Lesotho, while the poverty rate in poor areas of China would increase by 1 percentage point in the absence of migration and remittances (Du, Park, and Wang 2005). On a macro level, Adams and Page (2003) estimate the remittance elasticity of poverty to be of around –0.35. Our model predicts a slightly higher elasticity of –0.51.

Conclusions

Our analysis attempts to explain the role of migration and remittances in reducing poverty in Nepal between 1995 and 2003. We first examine the determinants of migration, remittances, and their impact on consumption. We identify the characteristics under which migrants are more likely to migrate, the incidence and level of remittances, and how household consumption is affected. We next turn to examining the effect migration and remittances have on poverty in Nepal.

The results indicate that migration and remittances have a strong impact on the living conditions of households with a migrant. The poverty rate among households with a member who migrates within Nepal would be twice as high as current levels if the migrant had stayed home. The poverty rate for households with a migrant working abroad would also be substantially higher had their members not migrated.

The results of our simulations show that almost 20 percent of the decline in poverty in Nepal between 1995 and 2004 can be attributed to increased work-related migration. In the absence of migration, the poverty rate in Nepal would increase from the currently observed 30.0 percent to 33.6 percent, and the mean per capita expenditure would decline from Nr 15,000 to Nr 14,000. Almost 58 percent of the aggregate increase in poverty could be accounted for by a higher number of the would-be poor among households with members who migrated internationally. Migration and remittances have only a marginal impact on income inequality in Nepal.

Our findings have important implications for public policy. The results emphasize the role of migration for work and remittance inflows in raising the living standards of recipient families and reducing aggregate poverty in Nepal. Moreover, the destination matters in determining the level and use of remittance flows, and therefore their potential for poverty reduction. Hence, strategies for economic growth and poverty reduction in Nepal should incorporate various aspects of the migration dynamics. Our results demonstrate that policies promoting both domestic migration and the export of labor—if such export were accompanied by remittances—could have an important effect on poverty reduction in

Nepal. Given that Nepal has such a plentiful supply of labor, migration for work provides employment and earning opportunities for a significant segment of the labor force. Unless the labor market situation changes dramatically, increasing numbers of Nepali men and women will seek job opportunities outside Nepal; migration and remittances could be expected to play an even greater role in the future economic development of the country.

Annex

Theoretical Model

We assume that utility of a household in state s can be linearly approximated as

$$U_{is} = X_i\gamma_s + Z_i\zeta_s + \eta_{is}, \ s = 1,2,3 \tag{1}$$

where Z_i is a vector of household characteristics that includes both X_i and z_i, γ and ζ are vectors of parameters, s is an indicator describing household migration choice, and η_{is} s are the error terms. The household selects the migration state s if

$$U_{is} > \max(U_{ij})_{j\neq s}, \ s = 1,2,3 \tag{2}$$

Consumption C_{is} in a particular state is observed only if that state is chosen:

$$C_{is} = \beta_s X_i + \mu_{is}, \ s = 1,2,3 \ \text{if} \ U_{is} > \max(U_{ij})_{j\neq s} \tag{3}$$

where β_s is a vector of parameters, and μ_{is} s are the error terms.

Some unobserved household and/or potential migrant's characteristics could affect both the household's decision to migrate (2) and the household's consumption (3).[6] For example, it might be optimal for a household to send a member with high entrepreneurial abilities abroad. These abilities, which are usually unobserved by a researcher, could also allow a migrant to earn higher wages in comparison with the average migrant worker and send more money back home. The challenge for our empirical strategy is to estimate the system of equations (1–3) controlling for such unobserved factors.

If error terms μ's and η's are not independent, the nonrandom selection of households into different states will result in a correlation between the explanatory variables X and errors μ's in equation (3). To obtain unbiased and consistent parameter estimates under an assumption of joint dependence of the error terms, we use the method of full information maximum likelihood (FIML). The method estimates the household consumption equations jointly with the equation describing the household choice of migration state allowing for the correlation of the error terms across equations.

To estimate the impact of remittances and migration on poverty and inequality in Nepal, we simulate the counterfactual expenditure distributions under different migration scenarios. The FIML estimation of equations (1–3) identifies the parameters of five-variate distribution of the error terms. The observed outcomes of the migration decision truncate the joint distribution of consumption for each individual. Though analytical expressions for such truncated distributions are unattainable, we recover the distributions by randomly drawing the error terms from the five-variate truncated normal with 1,000 replications. This way, we generate the simulated universe of 3,620,000 household expenditures with a different realization of conditional errors. The poverty rates and Gini coefficients (or any other statistic) could then be calculated for the particular counterfactual scenario (see Lokshin and Glinskaya (2008) for the description of estimation methodology).

Notes

1. The "Treaty of Peace and Friendship" signed by the Indian and Nepali governments in 1950 allowed Nepali nationals to enter India without a visa and work there with no restrictions (Thapliyal 1999).

2. The lagged asset index was constructed based on the estimated cash value of the flow of services provided by the durable goods. In our calculations, we included only durable assets purchased by households at least two years prior the date of the survey (2001 and older).

3. The results of the FIML estimation of equations are shown in Table 3.3 (discrete part of the model) and Table 3.4 (continuous part of the model). See the Annex for details on the model and equations.

4. To ascertain the validity of our instruments, we conduct a range of diagnostics tests. The hypothesis of no selection is strongly rejected by the Hausman (1978) test with $\chi^2 = 147.04$ and Prob $> \chi^2 = 0.0024$. The weak instrument test by Stock and Yogo (2002) shows that for the abroad migration instrument the hypothesis of weak instrument is rejected, the value of KP statistic is 39.466, and the critical values of Stock-Yogo test of 16.38 for 10 percent size of the Wald test. For the instrument of internal migration we obtain similar results.

5. The results of the 2001 Census show that Katmandu has the highest proportion of individuals born in other districts (37.8 percent). The majority of these migrants were born in rural areas (32.2 percent) and 4.8 percent of migrants in Katmandu come from other urban areas of Nepal (Central Bureau of Statistics 2003).

6. Migrant selection was studied by Chiswick (1978), and Borjas (1987, 1990, 1991) developed a model of self-selection based on unobserved migrant characteristics. The problem of self-selection of migrants was also studied by Docquier and Rapoport (1998), Aydemir (2003), and Kanbur and Rapoport (2005).

A recent study by McKenzie, Gibson, and Stillman (2006) concludes that migrants are positively selected in terms of both observed and unobserved skills.

References

Acharya, L. 2001. "Integration of Population in Poverty Alleviation Programmes in Nepal." In *Population and Development in Nepal,* ed. B. Kumar, Vol. 8, 57–66. Katmandu: Tribhuvan University.

Adams, R. 1989. "Worker Remittances and Inequality in Rural Egypt." *Economic Development and Cultural Change* 38: 45–71.

———. 1991. "The Economic Uses and Impact of International Remittances in Rural Egypt." *Economic Development and Cultural Change* 39: 695–722.

———. 1998. "Remittances, Investment and Rural Asset Accumulation in Pakistan." *Economic Development and Cultural Change* 47 (1): 155–73.

———. 2005. "Remittances, Household Expenditure, and Investment in Guatemala." Policy Research Working Paper 3532. World Bank, Washington, DC.

Adams, R., and J. Page. 2005. "Do International Migration and Remittances Reduce Poverty in Developing Countries?" *World Development* 33(10): 1645–69.

Agesa, R., and S. Kim. 2001. "Rural to Urban Migration as a Household Decision: Evidence from Kenya." *Review of Development Economics* 5(1): 60–75.

Alderman, H. 1996. "Savings and Economic Shocks in Rural Pakistan." *Journal of Development Economics* 51: 343–65.

Aydemir, A. 2003. "Are Immigrants Positively or Negatively Selected? The Role of Immigrant Selection Criteria and Self-Selection." Working Paper 0306002. Washington University, St. Louis.

Barham, B., and S. Bourcher. 1998. "Migration, Remittances, and Inequality: Estimating the Net Effects of Migration on Income Distribution." *Journal of Development Economics* 55: 307–31.

Bhattacharyya, B. 2005. "The Role of Family Decision in Internal Migration: The Case of India." *Journal of Development Economics* 18: 51–66.

Bhattrai, R. 2005. "Migration of Nepalese Youth for Foreign Employment: Problems and Prospects." Report. Youth Action Nepal, Katmandu.

———. 2007. "Open Borders, Closed Citizenship: Nepali Labor Migrants in Delhi." Report. South Asia Study Center, Delhi, India.

Borjas, G. 1987. "Self-Selection and the Earnings of Immigrants." *American Economic Review* 77(4): 531–51.

———. 1990. "Self-Selection and the Earnings of Immigrants: Reply." *American Economic Review* 80(1): 305–08.

———. 1991. "Immigration and Self-Selection." In *Immigration, Trade and the Labor Market*, ed. R. B. Freeman and J. Abowd, 29–76. Chicago: University of Chicago Press.

Carrington, W., E. Detragiache, and T. Vishwanath. 1996. "Migration with Endogenous Moving Costs." *American Economic Review* 86: 909–30.

Central Bureau of Statistics. 2003. "Population Census 2001: National Report." Central Bureau of Statistics, Katmandu.

Chhetry, D. 1999. "Caste/Ethnic Groups as Primary Units of Concern of Poverty." *Nepal Population Journal* 8(7): 43–48.

———. 2002. "Population, Development and Poverty in Nepal: An Integrated Approach of Analysis." In *Population and Development in Nepal*, ed. B. Kumar, Vol. 10, 72–83. Katmandu: Tribhuvan University.

Chiswick, B. 1978. "The Effect of Americanization on the Earnings of Foreign Born Men." *Journal of Political Economy* 88(3): 620–29.

Docquier, F., and H. Rapoport. 1998. "Are Migrant Minorities Strategically Self-Selected?" *Journal of Population Economics* 11: 579–88.

Du, Y., A. Park, and S. Wang. 2005. "Migration and Rural Poverty in China." *Journal of Comparative Economics* 33: 688–709.

Dustmann, C., and O. Kirchkamp. 2002. "The Optimal Migration Duration and Activity Choice after Re-migration." *Journal of Development Economics* 67: 351–72.

Efron, B. 1981. "Nonparametric Estimates of Standard Error: The Jackknife, the Bootstrap and Other Methods." *Biometrika* 68(3): 589–99.

Esquivel, Gerardo, and Alejandra Huerta-Pineda. 2007. "Remittances and Poverty in Mexico: A Propensity Score Matching Approach." *Integration and Trade Journal* 27: 45–71.

Fafchamps, M., and F. Shilpi. 2003. "The Spatial Division of Labor in Nepal." *Journal of Development Studies* 39(6): 23–66.

Funkhauser, E. 1992. "Mass Emigration, Remittances and Economic Adjustment: The Case of El Salvador in the 1980s." In *Migration and the Workforce: Economic Consequences for the United States*, ed. G. Borjas and R. Freeman, 135–76. Chicago: University of Chicago Press.

Gustafsson, B., and N. Makonnen. 1993. "Poverty and Remittances in Lesotho." *African Economies* 2(2): 49–73.

Jha, H. 1999. *Status of Informal Sector Workers: The Other Side of Economy in Nepal*. Katmandu: Centre for Economic and Technical Studies.

Hausman, J. 1978. "Specification Tests in Econometrics." *Econometrica* 46: 1251–71.

Heckman, J., and G. Sedlacek. 1990. "Self-Selection and the Distribution of Hourly Wages." *Journal of Labor Economics* 43(1, pt. II): S329–63.

Hildebrandt, N., and D. McKenzie. 2004. "The Effects of Migration on Child Health in Mexico." *Economia* 6(1): 257–89.

Hoddinott, J. 1994. "A Model of Migration and Remittances Applied to Western Kenya." *Oxford Economic Papers* 45: 135–51.

Kanbur, R., and H. Rapoport. 2005. "Migration Selectivity and the Evolution of Spatial Inequality." *Journal of Economic Geography* 5: 43–57.

Kollmair, M., S. Manandhar, B. Subedi, and S. Thieme. 2006. "New Figures for Old Stories: Migration and Remittances in Nepal." *Migration Letters* 3(2): 151–60.

Kumar, B. 2003. "Migration, Poverty and Development in Nepal." Paper presented for an Expert Group Meeting on Migration and Development, Economic and Social Commission for Asia and the Pacific, Bangkok, August 27–29, 2003.

Lokshin, Michael, and Elena Glinskaya. 2008. "The Effect of Male Migration for Work on Employment Patterns of Females in Nepal." Policy Research Working Paper 4757. World Bank, Washington, DC.

Low, A. 1986. *Agricultural Development in Southern Africa: Farm Household Economics and the Food Crisis.* London: James Curry.

McKenzie, D., J. Gibson, and S. Stillman. 2006. "How Important Is Selection? Experimental vs. Non-Experimental Measures of the Income Gains from Migration." IZA Discussion Paper 2087. Institute for the Study of Labor, Bonn.

———. 2007. "Moving to Opportunity, Leaving Behind What? Evaluating the Initial Effects of a Migration Policy on Incomes and Poverty in Source Areas." *New Zealand Economic Papers* 41(2): 197–224.

McKenzie, D., and H. Rapoport. 2005. "Migration Networks, Migration Incentives, and Education Inequality in Rural Mexico." Paper presented at the Inter-American Development Bank Conference "Economic Integration, Remittances, and Development," Washington, DC, February 2005.

Mesnard, A. 2004. "Temporary Migration and Capital Market Imperfections." *Oxford Economic Papers* 56: 242–62.

Mroz, T. 1999. "Discrete Factor Approximations in Simultaneous Equation Models: Estimating the Impact of a Dummy Endogenous Variable on a Continuous Outcome." *Journal of Econometrics* 92(2): 233–74.

Munshi, K. 2003. "Networks in the Modern Economy: Mexican Migrants in the U.S. Labor Market." *Quarterly Journal of Economics* 118(2): 549–99.

Nandini, A. 1999. "Engendered Mobilization—The Key to Livelihood Security: IFAD's Experience in South Asia." International Fund for Agricultural Development, Rome. http://www.ifad.org/hfs/thematic/southasia/south_toc .htm.

Sheddon, D. 2005. "Nepal's Dependence on Exporting Labor." Migration Policy Institute, Washington, DC. http://www.migrationinformation.org/Profiles/ display.cfm?id=277.

Sheddon, D., J. Adhikari, and G. Gurung. 2000. "Foreign Labor Migration and the Remittance Economy of Nepal." Report. DFID, Katmandu.

Stark, O. 1978. "Economic-Demographic Interaction in the Course of Agricultural Development: The Case of Rural-to-Urban Migration." Research Report 2/78, David Horowitz Institute for Research of Developing Countries, Tel Aviv.

———. 1991. *The Migration of Labor.* Cambridge, MA: Blackwell.

Stark, O., and D. Levhari. 1982. "On Migration and Risk in LDCs." *Economic Development and Cultural Change* 31: 191–96.

Stark, O., and R. Lucas. 1988. "Migration, Remittances, and the Family." *Economic Development and Cultural Change* 36(3): 465–81.

Stock, J., and M. Yogo. 2002. "Testing for Weak Instruments in Linear IV Regression." Technical Working Paper 284. National Bureau of Economic Research, Cambridge, MA.

Taylor, E., and J. Mora. 2006. "Does Migration Reshape Expenditures in Rural Household? Evidence from Mexico." Policy Research Working Paper 3842. World Bank, Washington, DC.

Taylor, E., S. Rozelle, and A. de Brauw. 2003. "Migration and Incomes in Source Communities: A New Economics of Migration Perspective from China." *Economic Development and Cultural Change* 52(1). University of Chicago Press, Chicago.

Taylor, E., and T. Wyatt. 1996. "The Shadow Value of Migrant Remittances, Income and Inequality in a Household-Farm Economy." *Journal of Development Studies* 32(6): 899–912.

Thapliyal, S. 1999. "Movement of Population between India and Nepal: Emerging Challenges." *Strategic Analysis* 23(5). http://www.ciaonet.org/olj/sa/sa_aug99.html.

Thieme, S. 2003. "Savings and Credit Associations and Remittances: The Case of Far West Nepalese Labor Migrants in Delhi, India." Working Paper 39. Employment Sector, International Labor Office, Geneva.

Thieme, S., R. Bhattrai, G. Gurung, M. Kollmair, S. Manandhar, and U. Muller-Boker. 2005. "Addressing the Needs of Nepalese Migrant Workers in Nepal and in Delhi, India." *Mountain Research and Development* 25(2): 109–14.

Woodruff, C., and R. Zenteno. 2001. "Remittances and Microenterprises in Mexico." Working paper. University of California in San Diego Graduate School of International Relations and Pacific Studies.

World Bank. 2004. "Nepal Development Policy Review: Restarting Growth and Poverty Reduction." Report 29382-NP, Poverty Reduction and Economic Management, South Asia Region. World Bank, Washington, DC.

———. 2006. "Nepal, Resilience Amidst Conflict: An Assessment of Poverty in Nepal, 1995–96 and 2003–04." Report 34843-NP, Poverty Reduction and

Economic Management Sector Unit, South Asia Region. World Bank, Washington, DC.

———. 2007. *World Development Report 2007: Development and the Next Generation*. Washington, DC: World Bank.

Yamanaka, K. 2000. "Nepalese Labour Migration to Japan: From Global Warriors to Global Workers." *Ethnic and Racial Studies* 23(1): 62–93.

Yang, D., and H. Choi. 2005. "Are Remittances Insurance? Evidence from Rainfall Shocks in the Philippines." Research Seminar in International Economics. Working Paper 535, University of Michigan, Ann Arbor.

CHAPTER 4

The Evolution of Albanian Migration and Its Role in Poverty Reduction

Carlo Azzarri, Gero Carletto, Benjamin Davis, and Alberto Zezza[1]

Introduction

Migration has emerged as the most common livelihood strategy in Albania for coping with unemployment and other economic difficulties brought on by the transition to a market economy since the early 1990s. Driven by dire economic conditions, and facilitated by geographic proximity and the lure of western affluence transmitted through Italian television, many Albanian households perceive migration, whether temporary or permanent, to be an effective strategy for improving their livelihoods.

Less than a decade after the fall of communist rule, the number of Albanians abroad swelled to at least 600,000 individuals (King and Vullnetari 2003), possibly as high as 800,000 (Barjaba 2000). More recent estimates put the figure at over one million (Government of Albania 2005). As the Albanian economy grew and poverty reduction began to take hold in the early twenty-first century, migration flows tapered in most parts of the country except from the poorer mountain region, as migrants from these remote areas—which had previously experienced less migration due to lack of communication and financial means—sought opportunities outside Albania.

The large migration flows to date contribute to the growing importance of remittances as a major source of income for many Albanian households, and for the national economy. Officially, private transfers are estimated to have reached US$1 billion in 2005, constituting 14 percent of GDP (IMF 2006). Remittances thus serve as the most important source of foreign exchange, almost twice as large as the value of exports, more than seven times the value of foreign aid, and almost five times the amount of foreign direct investment (FDI) in 2005. Remittances are particularly important in the mountain region, where households receive proportionally more remittances from migrants than their counterparts in other areas of the country.

Migration can impact sending households through a number of channels. Migration and the derived remittances are likely to have a positive direct income effect on consumption, as well as a positive indirect income effect through the potential relaxation of binding liquidity and insurance constraints and subsequent impact on production and investment decisions. The huge flows of remittances raise questions regarding their impact on recipient households, particularly in terms of the potential benefits in improving long-term welfare and reducing poverty.

The aim of this chapter is to assess the linkages between migration and poverty in Albania, to provide policymakers a better understanding of dynamics of this critical mechanism used by the poor to improve their livelihoods and cope with adverse circumstances. First, the chapter provides descriptive information on trends in migration, remittances, and poverty reduction in Albania. Second, more advanced statistical techniques are employed to gain a deeper understanding of the drivers and impacts of migration. The data used in the chapter are derived from the 2005 Albanian Living Standards Measurement Survey, and secondary sources.

International Migration Trends in the Albanian Context

For the purposes of this analysis we distinguish between current and past migration. Current migrants include all former household members who no longer live in the household and are currently abroad.[2] Temporary migrants are all household members who have been abroad for at least one month since 1990 and have now returned to live in the household. Of course, a current migrant may decide to return home at some point in the future, while a household member with past migration experience may decide to migrate permanently at some time in the future. The issue is particularly thorny for most recent migrants, who may still be in the process of making a final decision on where to settle. For this reason, we only include migration episodes and returns that have occurred up to December 2004, and we only consider migrants who have been abroad for at least six months (for current migrants), or who have returned at least six months before the survey (for temporary migrants).[3] We use the term "current migration" interchangeably with "permanent migration," and "past migration" interchangeably with "temporary migration."

Current Migration

International migration out of Albania over the past 15 years has been massive, relative to the nation's small population. One out of every three households in Albania (34 percent) has at least one former member currently living abroad, and about one-half of these households have more than one. Of the almost one million individuals who have split off from the original sample households since 1990, about one-half are currently living abroad. Of these, about 80 percent are equally divided between Greece and Italy, while the remaining 20 percent have migrated to other European destinations or farther afield to North America.

The sample design allows a regional analysis of migration patterns by coastal, central, mountain, and the capital city area, Tirana, as well as by urban versus rural location. Over 55 percent of permanent migrants originated in rural areas (Table 4.1). Although representing more than half of total migrants, rural adults have a lower propensity to migrate internationally on a permanent basis than their urban counterparts (42 versus 53 percent). Among all split-offs,[4] individuals in the urban coastal region, including the cities of Vlorë, Durrës, and Shkodër, are those with the highest propensity to migrate internationally (as opposed to leave the household but remain in Albania), while people from the poorer, rural mountain region are the least likely, with an incidence of 28 percent.

In terms of destination, a very small percentage of migrants from rural areas migrate to distant destinations beyond the neighboring countries of Greece and Italy. Almost 60 percent stay in Albania (versus less than 50 percent for individuals from urban areas), while the remainder migrate mostly to Greece and Italy. For individuals moving out of Tirana, one in four will choose a destination other than Greece and Italy.

Table 4.1 Prevalence of Migration by Residence of Original Household

	Population as of 1990		Permanent migrants		All split-offs		
	Number	Percent	Number	Percent	Number	Percent	Prevalence[a]
Tirana	389,452	12.7	47,489	10.5	92,965	9.6	0.511
Other urban	959,715	31.3	154,711	34.3	293,891	30.2	0.526
Rural	1,720,097	56	248,837	55.2	586,873	60.3	0.424
Tirana	389,452	12.7	47,489	10.5	92,965	9.6	0.511
Coastal urban	412,678	13.5	85,801	19.0	148,780	15.3	0.577
Coastal rural	544,820	17.8	114,214	25.3	242,692	24.9	0.471
Central urban	477,876	15.6	62,857	13.9	131,734	13.5	0.477
Central rural	896,242	29.2	113,242	25.1	268,739	27.6	0.421
Mountain urban	69,160	2.3	6,053	1.3	13,377	1.4	0.452
Mountain rural	279,035	9.1	21,381	4.7	75,442	7.8	0.283
Total	3,069,263	100	451,037	100	973,729	100	0.463

a. Prevalence is computed as the ratio between the total number of migrants and the total number of split-off individuals.

Conversely, one migrant in four from other urban centers moves to Italy. As expected, a higher share of migrants to Italy comes from coastal cities such as Vlorë and Durrës. Among the permanent migrants from urban areas in the mountain region, a higher percentage move to Italy than to Greece.

Over time, the flows of permanent migrants have fluctuated considerably, more than doubling after 1996, peaking in 2000 at about 50,000 new migrants per year, and steadily decreasing afterward (Figure 4.1).[5,6]

A large proportion of emigrants come from rural areas, and the gap between locations has increased over time. By 2002, migration from rural areas accounted for about two-thirds of total migration. The number of new migrants has dropped considerably over the past few years in all but the mountain region (Figure 4.2a). Looking at the shares of permanent migrants, the mountain region is the only one exhibiting a continuous upward trend, becoming steeper over the past several years (Figure 4.2b). By 2004 migrants from the mountain region represented over 10 percent of the stock of current migrants. It should be noted that despite this trend, the bulk of current migrants are still from the central and coastal region.

Greece and Italy are the destinations for about 40 percent of permanent migrants, but the pattern has fluctuated somewhat across the years, presumably in response to country-specific migration policies and other pull factors. Particularly revealing is the large increase of migration to Greece in the two years preceding the first regularization program in 1998—and coinciding with the years immediately following the collapse

Figure 4.1   Flow of Permanent Migrants, by Year of Migration

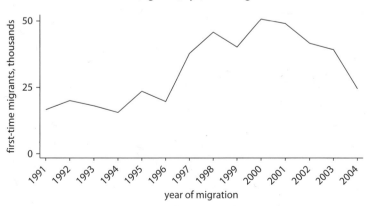

Figure 4.2   Permanent Migration by Region, 1991–2004

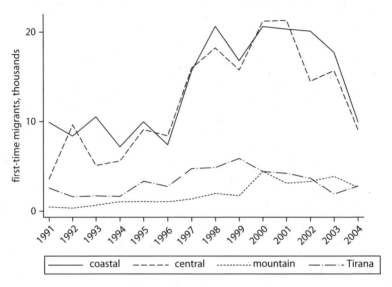

a. Flow of permanent migrants by region, 1991–2004

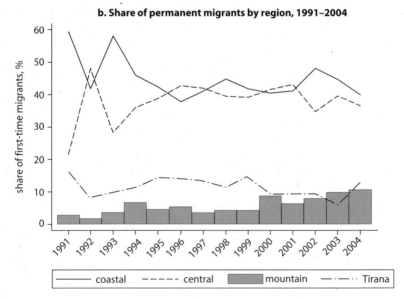

b. Share of permanent migrants by region, 1991–2004

of the Albanian financial pyramid scheme—followed by a drastic drop in 1999, when the proportion of migration to Italy and beyond was at its highest.

The same relationships can be seen in the total number of emigrants by year of migration and country of destination, as well as by the main regularization programs in Greece and Italy (Figure 4.3). In recent years, migrants tend to go even farther away than before. In 1999, Italy overtook Greece as the most popular destination for individuals moving abroad for the first time, though migration flows to this destination are steadily decreasing, particularly after the regularization program of 2002. Despite the downward trend of recent years following a peak migration in 2000, proportionately more people are now migrating to other destinations such as the United Kingdom and Germany, as well as North America. Presumably, migration becomes less onerous as migrant networks become more established abroad, allowing people to travel farther to more preferred destinations.

In comparison to the average adult left behind, permanent migrants are generally younger, male, and slightly more educated (Table 4.2). They are also more likely to come from female- and single-headed households.[7] As expected, migrants come from larger households (in 1990), which, also as a result of migration, are now significantly smaller. Similarly, households with migrants are on average less educated and older, partly

Figure 4.3   Destination of Current Migrants

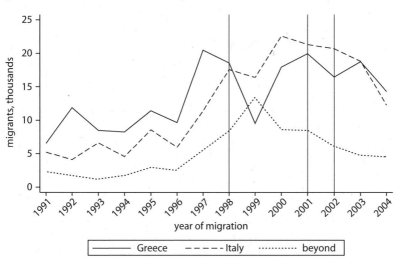

Note: The vertical bars represent major immigrant regularization programs in Greece.

Table 4.2   Characteristics of Current Migrants and Their Household of Origin

	Nonmigrant	Migrant	Total
Individual characteristics			
% of females	69**	35**	53
Age	36.6**	31.5**	34.2
Years of schooling	9.8**	10.1**	10.0
Household characteristics			
Poverty headcount (%)	21**	12**	19
Severe poverty	1.62**	0.61**	1.33
Poverty gap	4.7**	2.2**	4.0
Dependency ratio	0.84	0.81	0.83
Household size	4.5**	3.5**	4.2
Household size in 1990	5.1**	6.4**	5.5
Number of adults (age ≥ 15)	3.24**	2.93**	3.14
Number of adults in 1990	3.76**	5.81**	4.46
Head is female	0.08**	0.18**	0.11
Average adult years of education	9.23**	8.36**	8.93
Maximum adult years of education	11.1**	10.1**	10.8
Head is unemployed	0.05	0.04	0.04
Head is married	0.90**	0.84**	0.88
Head is widow/er	0.07**	0.15**	0.09
Head is single	0.10**	0.16**	0.12
Age of household head	48.5**	59.3**	52.1
Average age of adults in household	39.7**	46.3**	42.0

Note: ** = significant at the 5 percent level or lower.

as a result of the migration of the younger and more educated members in the household. Finally, households with a migrant abroad are also wealthier, as illustrated by the different poverty indicators, although clearly the causality direction is ambiguous.[8]

However, the demographic and socioeconomic makeup of permanent migrants is changing: older individuals, more women, and less educated individuals have begun migrating. These trends may have substantial implications in terms of future remittances as a consequence of the lower earning potential of these groups. A possible explanation for the increasing flow of women and older migrants is family reunification following recent regularization programs in the main destination countries. Interestingly, female migrants are on average more educated than men, particularly in the 1990s. The downward trend in educational levels does not concern the flow of permanent migrants moving from Tirana to destinations beyond Greece and Italy. For this particular flow, educational levels of migrants have remained stable over the years, at levels significantly above those going to Greece and Italy.

Temporary Migration

While working abroad, temporary migrants acquire skills and develop transnational social networks. Migrants returning to Albania bring these skills and networks with them, along with savings to invest. Findings from previous work in Albania have illustrated that past migration has a positive impact on the likelihood of owning a nonfarm business (Kilic et al. 2009). However, migrants often have to build up their skills and capital, and therefore recent returnees are likely to migrate again. Thus repeated temporary migration and subsequent settling in the origin country may act as an important component in reducing poverty and promoting growth within Albania.

Approximately 13 percent of adult individuals reported having spent at least one month abroad during the last 14 years, of which 53 percent are household heads. At the household level, this translates to about one in three households having had at least one episode of temporary migration since 1990. The vast majority of these households (82 percent) have had only one member abroad. Contrary to permanent migration, for which multiple siblings appear to be settling abroad, temporary migration thus seems to be generally taken up by only one household member. Temporary migrants are almost exclusively male, capturing both the male-dominated nature of the first wave of migration in the early 1990s and of seasonal/circular work migration, mainly to nearby Greece.

The temporary migration time trend reveals a bimodal distribution, with the two peaks corresponding to the initial opening of the borders in the early 1990s and the years immediately following the collapse of the pyramid scheme in 1996 (Figure 4.4).[9] This illustrates the use of migration as a coping mechanism. The peak in the early 1990s captures the massive emigration of those years; the majority of those emigrants eventually returned to Albania.

Although the number of temporary migrants going to nearby Greece has dropped significantly over the past few years, Greece remains by far the main destination of these temporary flows (Figure 4.5). Although not surprising, the magnitude of the differences among destinations, particularly relative to Italy, is remarkable. This is likely the result of multiple factors, including the characteristics of initial migrants and the conditions and policies in the host countries, which ultimately determined who stayed

Figure 4.4   Flow of First-Time, Temporary Migrants by Gender

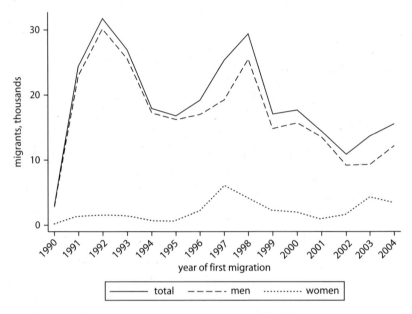

Figure 4.5   Flow of First-Time, Temporary Migrants by Destination

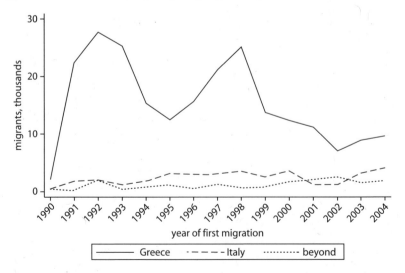

abroad (relatively fewer, and about equally divided between Greece and other destinations) and who returned (mostly from Greece).

A larger share of temporary migrants originates in rural areas, mostly from the central region close to the Greek border where a large proportion of Albanians of Greek descent live. Although to different degrees, all areas experienced increases in outflows in the periods after the opening of the borders and the collapse of the pyramid scheme. Emigration from the mountain region has continued at a slow and steady pace, passing Tirana in 1999 in terms of annual migrants and now close to emigration levels from the coastal areas (Figure 4.6a, b).

Temporary, short-term migrants are mainly younger, married, slightly more educated men from male-headed and larger households (Table 4.3). On average, they have migrated about four times in a 14-year period for a total of 26 months.[10] Similar to permanent flows, education levels of temporary migrants have been declining over time, while the average age of migrants has increased. The trend is indicative of an intensification of push factors, inducing migration of less suitable candidates.

Remittances

The importance of remittances in the Albanian economy cannot be overemphasized. Over the past several years, remittances have emerged as one of the key components of households' livelihood strategies. In 2005 remittances represented 14 percent of GDP (IMF 2006) and 13 percent of household income. The Albania Living Standards Measurement Survey 2005 (ALSMS05) collected remittance information at the individual level for all split-off adults who sent remittance to their households in the 12 months preceding the survey. In addition, in a separate module, it also collected information on all other private transfers received from abroad by the households from any other individual during the same reference period. Obviously individuals in the first group are the most likely to send remittances, given the stronger familial relationship.

Out of an estimated 451,000 split-off migrants,[11] approximately two-thirds (64.8 percent) made cash or in-kind remittances the year prior to the survey (Figure 4.7). On average, each sent US$1,179, for a total amount remitted of more than US$340 million in a 12-month period. This represents approximately 87 percent of total remittances received by all households in the same period. More distant relatives and friends sent the remaining share. Albanian households received a total of approximately US$400 million over a period of one year. These flows do not include all

Figure 4.6   Flow of First-Time, Temporary Migrants

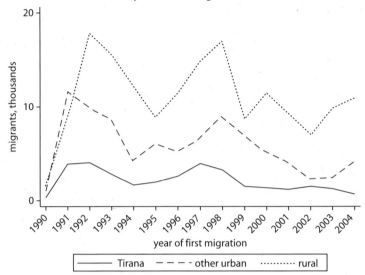

a. By location of original household

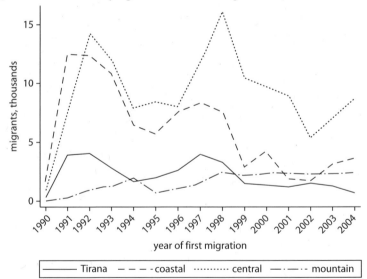

b. By region of residence of original household

Table 4.3   Characteristics of Temporary Migrants and Their Families

	Nonmigrants	Migrants	Total
% of females	58**	12**	52
Age	41.8**	37.8**	41.3
Years of education	8.7**	10.1**	8.92
Poverty headcount (%)	18	19	19
Severe poverty	1.32	1.35	1.33
Poverty gap	3.98	4.04	4
Unemployment ratio, last week	0.11	0.09	0.1
Dependency ratio	0.82	0.84	0.83
Household size	3.93**	4.71**	4.18
Number of adults (age ≥ 15)	2.98**	3.45**	3.14
Head is female	0.14**	0.06**	0.11
Average adult years of education	8.82**	9.17**	8.93
Maximum adult years of education	10.58**	11.11**	10.75
Head is unemployed	0.05	0.04	0.04
Head is married	0.86**	0.92**	0.88
Head is widow/er	0.11**	0.07**	0.09
Head is single	0.14**	0.08**	0.12

Note: ** = significant at 5 percent or lower.

Figure 4.7   Migrants and Remitters by Region, 2005

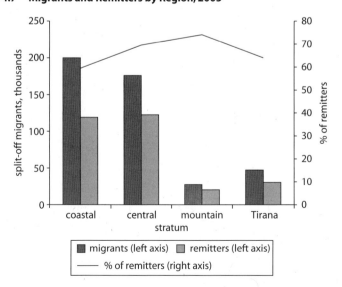

foreign earnings and savings brought back in person by migrants. Overall, compared with 2002, in 2005 a higher percentage of households received remittances, but on average each household received less. The total flow of remittances in 2005 increased by about 11 percent compared to 2002.

The mountain region appears to be benefiting disproportionately from remittances compared to other regions of the country, although in absolute numbers the majority of remittances go to the coastal and central region— origin of most permanent migration. Proportionately more migrants from the mountain region send remittances (74 percent versus less than 60 percent among split-offs from the coastal region). Moreover, migrants from the poorer mountain region send on average almost twice as much as migrants from the central region (Figure 4.8). Thus proportionately more and larger remittances are flowing into the poorer mountain region compared with other areas of the country. These findings, combined with the upward trend of international migration out of poorer mountain areas, points to a potentially increasing role of migration and remittances for poverty reduction in these more remote areas, which, until recently, appeared to have been cut off from the main migration flows toward international destinations.

Not surprisingly, a high percentage of households from the coastal region receive remittances from Italy (about 50 percent), while two-thirds of remittances to Tirana come from destinations other than Greece and Italy (Table 4.4). Among households in the mountain region receiving remittances, more than one-half receive transfers from destinations other than Greece. In terms of average amounts remitted, no significant

Figure 4.8   Mean Amount Remitted by Region, 2005

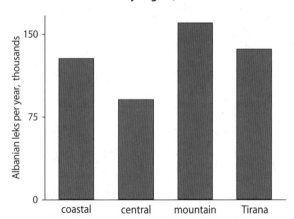

Table 4.4   Remittances by Destination and Region of Original Household Residence, 2005

Stratum	% of households receiving remittances from			Average amount remitted to household (2005 prices, leks)		
	Greece	Italy	Beyond	Greece	Italy	Beyond
Coastal	8	13	4	177,359	169,902	139,025
Central	10	5	4	145,910	148,956	182,782
Mountain	7	5	3	198,771	243,796	217,775
Tirana	2	4	9	239,100	150,299	187,398
Total	8	8	4	164,144	166,538	175,552

differences are observed across countries of residence of the migrant, while some variability is reported across regions of residence of the recipient households in Albania.

As expected, the length of migration has a notable impact both on the share of remitters and the value remitted by these migrants. Although fewer in number, a higher share of early migrants is still sending remittances. Based on their year of first migration, the share of migrants that remit increases up to 1997 before beginning to decline steadily. Only about 50 percent of the most recent migrants are sending remittances, versus more than 70 percent among those who left in the mid-1990s. These late migrants, however, are sending more on average (about US$300 more in the year preceding the survey). This is consistent with the finding that mountain region migrants, who are continuing to increase in number, are sending larger remittances. This finding also suggests that a very large share of split-offs maintain strong links with the sending households even after more than a decade, and they still send a steady, although on average smaller, stream of resources.[12] Conversely, a larger share of new migrants may find it difficult to start remitting right away, given the high initial costs of settlement in the host country.

The number of migrants and remitters are strongly and positively correlated with welfare: a significantly higher share of households in the top per capita expenditure quintiles have migrants abroad and receive remittances compared with their counterparts in the lower quintiles (Figure 4.9a). The overall trend between welfare level and the share of migrants sending remittances in each quintile, however, is virtually flat. Moreover, no difference exists across welfare quintiles in the average amount sent by split-off migrants (Figure 4.9b).

Figure 4.9   Migrants and Remitters: Household Comparisons

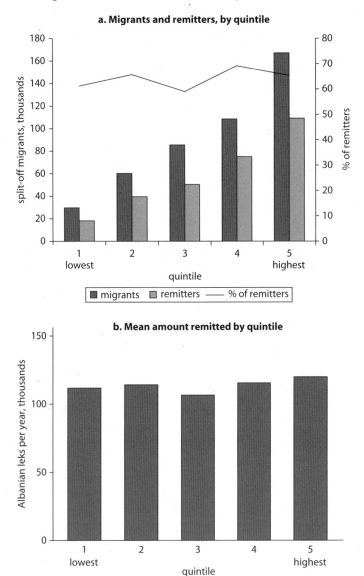

a. Migrants and remitters, by quintile

b. Mean amount remitted by quintile

In the above figures, the consumption levels, and thus the quintiles, are clearly affected by the level of remittances received. Utilizing household asset position avoids this endogeneity problem, although it is an imperfect proxy for household income.[13] Households in the middle of the asset distribution are the least likely to receive remittances

(Figure 4.10a). Better-off households (in 1990) are also receiving sub-stantially more, on average (Figure 4.10b).

The relation between the amounts remitted and the age of the split-off remitters reveals a U-shaped curve: migrants between the

Figure 4.10   Remittances and Household Assets

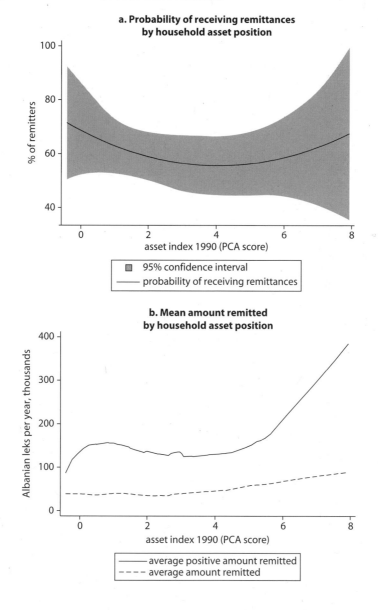

a. Probability of receiving remittances by household asset position

% of remitters

asset index 1990 (PCA score)

■ 95% confidence interval
— probability of receiving remittances

b. Mean amount remitted by household asset position

Albanian leks per year, thousands

asset index 1990 (PCA score)

—— average positive amount remitted
- - - average amount remitted

ages of 30–35 remit on average lower amounts (Figure 4.11a). Surprisingly, migrants in their early twenties remit on average the highest amounts. This is also the group, however, with the lowest share of remitters (Figure 4.11b). For the remaining age groups, the propensity to remit is virtually identical at around 65 percent. Thus the overall propensity to transfer money to members of the original households appears to be affected more by the number of years spent abroad and location of the household, and less by the age of the migrant (apart from the youngest).

Figure 4.11   Remittances by Age of Migrant

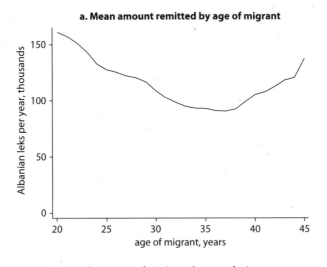

a. Mean amount remitted by age of migrant

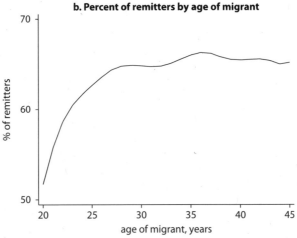

b. Percent of remitters by age of migrant

Remittance Flows and Poverty Reduction

Poverty rates in Albania have dropped by 7 percentage points in the short span of only three years, from a head count of 25.4 percent in 2002 to 18.5 percent in 2005 (World Bank 2007). The large geographic variations in poverty of 2002 have undergone dramatic changes, particularly as a result of the large poverty reduction in the rural mountain region, and to a lesser extent in Tirana and other urban areas (Table 4.5). In 2002, the rural poverty rate in the mountain region was double that of the national average. By 2005, this decreased to only about 50 percent above the national poverty rate.

Mapping the estimated poverty changes in the 2002–05 period against the levels and changes in remittance inflows into each region reveals some correlation. Tirana and the rural mountain regions show the largest increases in the share of households receiving remittances (Table 4.6). The shares are also matched by equally large increases in the total flows in monetary terms, with flows to Tirana more than doubling and the mountain region exhibiting increases of about 50 percent.

Proportionately more migrants from the poorer mountain region are sending remittances, and on average they are sending more. Furthermore, the mountain region is the only region in which the flow of new permanent migrants has been monotonically increasing over the past several years. Finally, the higher purchasing power of remittances to the mountain region compared with other regions may potentially amplify the impact of transfers in terms of poverty reduction. This evidence seems to suggest a possible link between migration and the large improvements in poverty reduction observed in the mountain region over the past few years.

Table 4.5 Poverty 2002–05 by Region

Region	Poverty headcount (%)			Poverty gap		
	2002	2005	Change	2002	2005	Change
Tirana	18	8	−9.7	3.77	1.65	−2.1
Coastal urban	20	17	−8.6	5.43	1.99	−3.4
Coastal rural	21	20	−1.2	3.62	4.06	0.4
Central urban	19	13	−6.8	3.82	2.99	−0.8
Central rural	29	26	−2.6	6.55	6.01	−0.5
Mountain urban	25	17	−7.6	6.52	3.61	−2.9
Mountain rural	50	28	−21.8	12.30	5.50	−6.8
Total	25	19	−6.9	5.71	4.00	−1.7

Table 4.6　Migrants and Remittances 2002–05 by Region

Region	% of households receiving remittances			Average amount remitted to household (2005 prices, leks)			Total amount remitted to household (2005 prices, billion leks)		
	2002	2005	Change	2002	2005	% change	2002	2005	% change
Tirana	15.8	31.0	15.2	160,537	181,715	13.2	2.3	5.8	152.2
Coastal urban	35.1	39.7	4.6	133,837	161,305	20.5	4.9	6.9	40.8
Coastal rural	30.2	38.7	8.5	208,922	196,807	–5.8	7.9	9.6	21.5
Central urban	31.8	29.3	–2.5	116,385	113,668	–2.3	4.4	4.2	–4.5
Central rural	31.0	33.3	2.3	193,539	136,055	–29.7	13.0	9.2	–29.2
Mountain urban	11.7	21.0	9.3	230,604	194,195	–15.8	0.4	0.7	47.7
Mountain rural	15.0	24.9	9.9	213,191	212,011	–0.6	1.8	2.8	55.6
Total	28	33	5.3	170,155	160,154	–5.9	35.0	39.0	11.4

Assessing the Impact of Migration on Poverty

A multivariate comparison based on the different types of migration reveals sizable differences in consumption levels, as well as poverty incidence and depth, between households with a current migrant abroad, and those without (Table 4.7). The same comparison based on temporary migration experience indicates no such significant differences. It would be misleading, however, to conclude that while current migration has had a positive impact on consumption and poverty, temporary migration has not.[14] It could be the case, for example, that permanent migrants had higher consumption levels even before migration, or that a household with temporary migrants had significantly lower consumption levels prior to migration compared with their nonmigrant counterparts.

The ALSMS05 contained a module on subjective poverty, in which a respondent per household (generally the household head) was asked to rank his or her perception of personal welfare at different points in time since 1990, based on a 10-rung ladder (1 = poorest).[15] Based on this information and household migration exposure, we draw a number of graphs to visually describe the relation between migration and changes in welfare, as perceived by the respondent. Comparing nonmigrant and migrant (any destination) households, no significant differences can be detected in either of the 1990 curves or the 2005 nonmigrant curve (Figure 4.12). However, the shift to the right of the fourth line is indicative of perceived improvements in 2005 by migrant households.

Similar conclusions can be drawn by considering current migration only, indicating that much of the perceived improvement is derived from this type of migration and not from temporary migration (Figure 4.13).

Disaggregating by destination, households with migrants to Greece perceived their situation somewhat improved, while the largest shift is for

Table 4.7   Poverty Indicators and Migration

	Permanent migration			Temporary migration			
	No	Yes	Change	No	Yes	Change	Total
Per capita consumption[a]	8,813	9,856	1,043***	9,202	8,943	−259	9,109
Poverty headcount	21.2	11.8	−9.4***	18.6	18.4	−0.1	18.5
Poverty gap	4.7	2.2	−2.5***	4.0	4.0	0.0	4.0
Number of observations	2,486	1,154		2,544	1,096		3,640

Note: *** = Significant at 1%.
a. Computed at the individual level.

Figure 4.12   Subjective Poverty Ladder in 1990 and 2005, with or without Any Migration

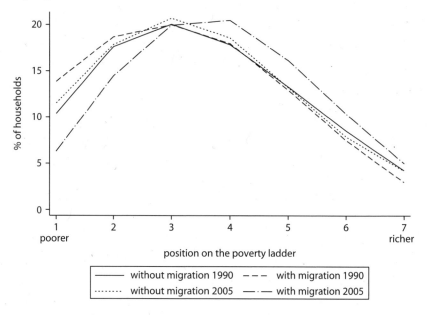

Figure 4.13   Subjective Poverty Ladder in 1990 and 2005, with or without Current Migration

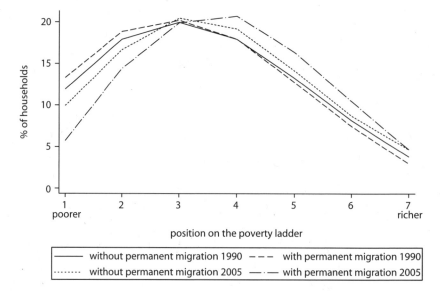

household with migrants to Italy and beyond (Figure 4.14). This may reflect the potentially higher returns and status associated with the latter type of migration, although, as observed earlier, migrants in these countries are not remitting significantly more than their counterparts in Greece.

Measuring the Impact of Migration on Poverty: An Instrumental Variable Approach

Descriptive statistics of both objective and subjective measures of welfare indicate that migration, particularly current migration to farther destinations, appears to have exerted a positive impact on welfare among migrant households at the origin. However, the decision to migrate is not random, and is likely to be associated with a number of observable and unobservable characteristics of the migrants, as well as of the household and the local environment where they live or moved. To properly identify the impact of migration, ideally we would have longitudinal data capturing conditions before and after for a group of migrants as well as for a control group. Our available data fall far short of these requirements.

For this reason, an alternative estimation strategy is proposed, based on the instrumental variable (IV) technique. We estimate a log-consumption model in which, given the likely endogeneity of the migration variable, we instrument separately for both temporary and permanent migration using

Figure 4.14   Subjective Poverty Ladder in 1990 and 2005, with or without Permanent Migration by Destination Country

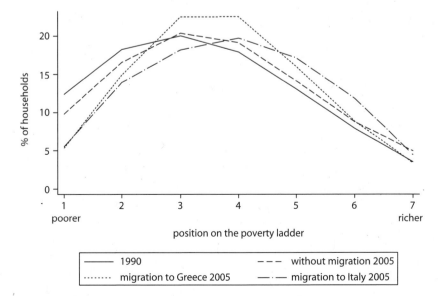

a number of variables chosen from a set of potential candidates contained in the survey. Thorough diagnostic testing is carried out to assess both the relevance and strength of our instruments. The strategy is to use IV estimators clustered at the primary sampling unit (PSU) level to take intragroup correlation into account. We instrument and estimate separate models at the household level for temporary and permanent migration. Explanations of the models and full estimation of results, including coefficients and the robust standard errors of both the ordinary least squares (OLS) and the corresponding IV specification, are found in the Annex.

Contrary to the descriptive results, which showed an insignificant difference in consumption levels across groups, both OLS and IV models clearly point to a positive and significant relationship between temporary migration and welfare. The estimated IV coefficient of the instrumented migration variable indicates that one additional year of international migration is associated with a 5 percent increase in consumption. This IV impact is somewhat larger than the one implied by the OLS coefficient, suggesting a negative bias in the temporary migration process. The model also finds that larger household size, remoteness (according to a distance index), and living in a region outside of Tirana are all associated with lower consumption, while education is positively correlated with consumption.

The impact on consumption is also positive and significant for permanent migration. Although the large magnitude of the IV coefficient is somewhat suspicious, both estimations are indicative of strong causality between having a permanent migrant living abroad and household consumption levels. Having a migrant abroad is associated with an increase in consumption of about 50 percent. Most of the other variables have qualitatively similar results as previous model on temporary migration. Among the most salient differences are the now significant (and negative) coefficients on the age of the household head and the unemployment rate at the local level.

Overall, a positive association between migration and welfare appears to exist, irrespective of migration type. The magnitude of the impact is quite different, however, with permanent migration having a much stronger effect on welfare.

Conclusion

Migration in Albania continues to be a very dynamic and pervasive phenomenon, with the majority of Albanian households experiencing some form of migration since 1990, and one-third of households having at least one household member currently living abroad. Striking changes in both the magnitude and composition of the flows are still occurring at an impressive pace, with new patterns emerging over the past several years and old patterns stabilizing or transforming in response to conditions at home, in the main host countries, and as part of a natural maturation of the migration process.

While Greece remains the main destination of temporary migrants, Italy and farther destinations represent a higher share of longer-term migration. Particularly interesting is the trend to destinations in northern Europe and North America, which continue to attract an increasingly higher number of the most educated and skilled individuals. The demographic and socioeconomic characteristics of this group of migrants differ from the rest of migrants who, on average, are increasingly less educated and older.

International migration appears to be slowing, as a more stable economic environment contributes to stabilizing migration flows. The downward trend in permanent migration flows is shared by all regions with the exception of the poorer mountain region. Compared with the 1990s, proportionately more permanent migrants—the more lucrative form of migration—are coming from the mountain region. Over half of the remittances received are from beyond Greece, either Italy or farther afield. Moreover, migrants from the mountain region have a higher propensity to remit, and on average remit more.

Both descriptive statistics and OLS/instrumental variable analysis find solid evidence indicating that both temporary and permanent migration have significant positive impacts on household consumption and poverty rates. Controlling for other socioeconomic characteristics, an additional year of temporary international migration is associated with a 5 percent increase in consumption for the sending household, while having a permanent migrant abroad is associated with a 50 percent increase in household consumption.

The poverty reduction potential of these relatively new flows of migrants, and the resulting remittances back home, is enormous. Some of these effects may already be at work, as reflected in the progress in poverty reduction achieved by the mountain region over the past few years. As proportionately more migrants originate in the poorer areas and more remittances are flowing toward poorer regions, the poverty reduction impact of migration may broaden in the future.

Annex

Variable Description

In all models, the dependent variable is the household's log per capita consumption. A brief explanation of the independent variables used in both models is presented below. Descriptive statistics of the main variables, by migration status, are found in Tables 4A.1 and 4A.2.

Table 4A.1   Selected Descriptive Statistics by Permanent Migration Status

Variable	Without permanent migration	With permanent migration	Total	Signif.
Per capita consumption	8,813	9,856	9,109	***
Tirana	0.15	0.12	0.14	***
Coastal urban	0.13	0.18	0.15	***
Coastal rural	0.14	0.24	0.17	***
Central urban	0.18	0.15	0.17	**
Central rural	0.30	0.24	0.28	***
Mountain urban	0.03	0.02	0.02	*
Mountain rural	0.08	0.05	0.07	***
Number of children ≤5 yrs old	0.40	0.19	0.33	***
Household size	4.54	3.48	4.18	***
Age of household head	48	59	52	***
Head is female	0.08	0.18	0.11	***
Average adult years of education	9.2	8.4	8.9	***
Unemployment rate 2002 (at the district level)	12.79	13.29	12.96	**
PCA score index 1990	−0.03	0.28	0.08	***
Household Distant Index	0.02	−0.02	0	
Household Social Capital Index	−0.01	0.02	0	
Total months abroad 1990–2004 in household	10.55	9.11	10.06	
Anyone spoke Greek in 1990	0.1	0.1	0.1	***
Household had family friends or relatives abroad in 1990	0.08	0.08	0.08	
Number of individuals living abroad in household	0.00	1.80	0.61	***
% of males 20–39 by municipality	13.96	13.54	13.82	***
Dummy: anyone spoke Greek or Italian in 1990	0.1	0.3	0.2	***
Number of observations	2,400	1,240	3640	
Percent	66	34	100	

Note: Significance level: * = 10%; ** = 5%; *** = 1%.

Table 4A.2   Selected Descriptive Statistics by Temporary Migration Status

Variable	Without temporary migration	With temporary migration	Total	Signif.
Per capita consumption	9,202	8,943	9,109	
Tirana	0.16	0.10	0.14	***
Coastal urban	0.15	0.15	0.15	
Coastal rural	0.17	0.18	0.17	
Central urban	0.18	0.15	0.17	***
Central rural	0.25	0.33	0.28	***
Mountain urban	0.02	0.02	0.02	*
Mountain rural	0.07	0.07	0.07	
Number of children ≤5 yrs old	0.25	0.50	0.33	***
Household size	3.94	4.70	4.18	***
Age of household head	53	50	52	***
Head is female	0.14	0.06	0.11	***
Average adult years of education	8.8	9.2	8.9	***
Unemployment rate 2002 (at the district level)	13.2	12.5	13.0	***
PCA score index 1990	0.05	0.13	0.08	
Household Distant Index	−0.01	0.03	0	
Household Social Capital Index	0.02	−0.04	0	
Total months abroad 1990–2004 in household	0.00	31.30	10.06	***
Anyone spoke Greek in 1990	0.04	0.11	0.06	***
Household had family friends or relatives abroad in 1990	0.07	0.10	0.08	***
Number of individuals living abroad in household	0.69	0.46	0.61	***
% of males 20–39 by municipality	13.71	14.04	13.82	***
Dummy: anyone spoke Greek or Italian in 1990	0.2	0.2	0.2	*
Number of observations	2,470	1,170	3640	
Percent	68	32	100	

Note: Significance level: * = 10%; ** = 5%; *** = 1%.

Migration

In the permanent migration model, the variable indicates the number of household split-offs living abroad. In the temporary migration model, the instrumented variable measures the total number of months spent abroad over the period 1990–2004 by any current household member. Both variables are instrumented separately, using the exclusion restrictions described below (see table 4A.3).

Table 4A.3   Log per Capita Consumption Estimations: Measuring the Impact of Migration

	Temporary migration		Permanent migration	
	OLS	IV	OLS	IV
(District dummies omitted)				
Number of children ≤5 yrs old	−0.087***	−0.098***	−0.086***	−0.124***
	[0.012]	[0.014]	[0.013]	[0.019]
Household size	−0.253***	−0.255***	−0.242***	−0.130***
	[0.013]	[0.016]	[0.013]	[0.037]
Household size squared	0.014***	0.014***	0.014***	0.008***
	[0.001]	[0.002]	[0.001]	[0.002]
Age of household head	0.001	0.002	−0.003	−0.036***
	[0.004]	[0.004]	[0.004]	[0.010]
Age of household head squared	0	0	0	0.000***
	[0.000]	[0.000]	[0.000]	[0.000]
Head is female	−0.021	−0.019	−0.021	−0.009
	[0.024]	[0.024]	[0.024]	[0.033]
Average adult years of education	0.051***	0.049***	0.053***	0.065***
	[0.003]	[0.003]	[0.003]	[0.005]
PCA score index 1990	0.049***	0.046***	0.049***	0.044***
	[0.006]	[0.006]	[0.006]	[0.008]
Unemployment rate in 2002	−0.006***	−0.006***	−0.007***	−0.011***
(at the district level)	[0.002]	[0.002]	[0.002]	[0.003]
Household Distant Index	−0.035***	−0.036***	−0.035***	−0.034***
	[0.009]	[0.010]	[0.009]	[0.009]
Household Social Capital Index	−0.038***	−0.038***	−0.037***	−0.039***
	[0.008]	[0.008]	[0.008]	[0.010]
Total months abroad	0.001***	0.005**		
1990–2004 in household	[0.000]	[0.002]		
Number of individuals living			0.034***	0.409***
abroad in household			[0.008]	[0.105]
Constant	9.445***	9.403***	9.505***	9.964***
	[0.114]	[0.119]	[0.116]	[0.188]
Observations	3638	3638	3638	3638
Adjusted R-squared	0.48	0.45	0.48	0.10
F test of excluded instruments		11.45		15.68
Anderson-Rubin chi-squared test				
of endogenous regressors		7.90		36.30
p-value		0.02		0.00
Cragg-Donald F-stat		39.14		22.25
Cragg-Donald chi-squared		79.32		45.10
p-value		0.00		0.00
Hansen J-statistic		0.21		2.30
p-value		0.65		0.13

(continued)

Table 4A.3   Log per Capita Consumption Estimations: Measuring the Impact of Migration *(continued)*

	Temporary migration		Permanent migration	
	OLS	IV	OLS	IV
Anderson canonical correlation				
LR chi-squared test		78.47		44.82
p-value		0.00		0.00

Note: Robust standard errors in brackets. *** = significant at 1%.
Excluded instruments
For temporary: anyone in household who spoke Greek in 1990; household had relatives or family friends living abroad in 1990.
For permanent: Percent of males 20–39 by municipality; anyone in household who spoke Italian or Greek in 1990.

The permanent migration variable is instrumented using two variables: (1) the proportion of males between the age of 20 and 39 in the community, and (2) whether any member of the household spoke either Greek or Italian in 1990. The commune/municipality-level proportion of the male population aged 20 to 39, which was computed from the 2001 Population Census, varies quite dramatically across areas.[16] To the extent that lower proportions capture the density of migration within a commune, we expect that this proxy of the access to extended migration networks abroad, and consequently lower information costs, will be correlated with household migration decision.

Knowledge of either Greek or Italian—the languages spoken in the two primary destination countries—by any household member in 1990, besides making the destination country more attractive by lowering the costs of assimilation, is also indicative of affinity in culture and mentality, as well as geographic proximity. This familiarity with the language spoken in the host country has been noted to be an important factor in determining the direction of migration in Albania (de Zwager et al. 2005). Consequently, mostly Orthodox Christian Albanians come from the southern and southeastern regions of the country, where a sizeable ethnic Greek minority has historically resided or migrated to Greece. Italy serves as the preferred destination for Albanians from the central and coastal regions, where the Italian TV channels and way of life are most popular (de Zwager et al. 2005). Exposure to Greek and Italian languages in 1990 was consistently dependent on location and cultural background. Also, it was mainly induced by exogenous factors—such as the presence of ethnic Greek minorities and Italian television—and not due to a reflection of differences in wealth, education, or entrepreneurial skills in the pre-1990 period. These factors suggest that knowledge of languages in 1990 may fulfill the requirement of instrumental exogeneity.

The temporary migration variable is instrumented using two different instruments: (1) whether any household member spoke Greek in 1990 and (2) whether the household had any relatives or family friends living abroad in 1990. Regarding the language instrument, a similar argument made above also applies. However, contrary to permanent migration, the bulk of temporary migration has traditionally been to Greece, partly due to its vicinity and porous borders. Thus we use knowledge of the Greek language in 1990 to identify the decision to migrate temporarily. Finally, we use a proxy variable for past migration exposure at the household level, likely to be correlated with actual migration. By using this variable we hope to capture potential network effects, expected to lower the cost of migration.

Household-Level Variables

In each model, we control for a number of household-level characteristics, including household size (in quadratic form), the number of children below five years of age, the age and gender of the household head, the average years of education of all adult members, as well as a proxy variable for wealth in 1990. We also construct a distance index and a social capital index for each household. In the first index we consider the distance to three basic services, as reported by the households: the walking distance from the nearest primary school, health clinic or doctor, and bus station. The social capital index is constructed using data on: (1) the total number of people on whom the respondent can rely in times of need; (2) the extent to which the respondent believes others in the community are willing to help each other out (on a 5-point scale), and (3) the extent to which the respondent feels that differences among community members divide the community (also on a 5-point scale). We then performed a factor analysis on these three responses, and took the first factor score to create the index.

Community and Spatial Variables

We control for a number of factors at different levels of spatial aggregation. These include the unemployment rate at the district level (in 2002) and the location of the households in relation to one of the 36 districts (with Tirana used as the reference group), though the estimated parameters are not shown in the tables.

IV Testing

The instruments described above were chosen from a pool of candidates and their choice was assessed through comprehensive diagnostics. Results of the diagnostic tests are reported at the bottom of the estimation tables. First, we formally check for the endogeneity of the migration variable to be instrumented using the Anderson-Rubin test. A rejection of the null means that the coefficient of the endogenous regressor is statistically different from zero in the structural equation.

The over-identification of instruments is tested using the heteroskedasticity-robust Hansen-J statistic. The statistic allows observations to be correlated within groups. The joint null hypothesis is that the instruments are valid instruments, that is, uncorrelated with the error term, and that the tested instruments have to be correctly excluded from the estimated equation. Under the null, the test statistic is distributed as a chi-squared in the number of over-identifying restrictions. A rejection of the null hypothesis indicates that either the instrumental variables are wrongly excluded from the regression, or the orthogonality condition is not satisfied, thus casting doubt on the validity of the chosen instruments. We also run the Anderson canonical correlations likelihood-ratio test to further check whether the equation is identified, that is, that the excluded instruments are relevant. The statistic provides a measure of instrument relevance, and rejection of the null indicates that the model is identified.

An instrument, though valid, may still be "weak." The consequence of using instruments with little explanatory power is a larger bias in the estimated IV coefficients (Hahn and Hausman 2003), thus potentially rendering the use of instrumented models less beneficial relative to uninstrumented estimators. For this purpose, we also run the Cragg-Donald's joint significance F-test of the instruments in the first stage regression to test for their relevance. As suggested in the literature (Steiger and Stock 1997), as a rule of thumb we use a value of above 10 of the F statistic to conclude with some confidence that the chosen instruments are "strong."

Notes

1. We would like to acknowledge Jennica Larrison for useful comments on an earlier version of the paper.

2. The survey collected information on all sons and daughters of the household head and/or the spouse older than 15, as well as the spouse if he/she is no

longer living in the household and residing abroad. Sons and daughters account for about 98 percent of the total number.

3. For the same reason, figures relative to more recent years, and particularly 2004, should be interpreted with caution; as for these recent migrants, the distinction between permanent and temporary might be less clear cut.

4. Split-off adults are members of nuclear households who since 1990 have left to live elsewhere.

5. In this and the following figures, the year indicates the year of first migration of permanent migrants. Thus, in case of multiple events prior to settling abroad, we use the timing of the first of such events. However, in the majority of cases, permanent migrants only reported one migration episode. Also, the lower numbers in the early 1990s reflect the fact that a higher number of these early migrants have now returned and settled back in Albania, as reflected in the high numbers of temporary migrants in these early years of transition (see next section).

6. This downward trend is particularly relevant to the current policy debate: is migration in Albania as a whole truly tapering off? Is the improving economic situation driving the recent downward trend? This chapter does not address these questions.

7. If we only consider sons and daughters abroad to classify migrant households, the proportion of female-headed households drops to 13 percent, compared with 18 percent in Table 4.2, which also considers migrant spouses.

8. On the one hand, poverty might be hypothesized to cause migration; on the other hand, only the more wealthy households may be able to afford migration, particularly to more distant destinations. Furthermore, returns to migration, largely in the form of remittances, lift households out of poverty. Some of these issues are further explored in McKenzie and Sasin (2007), and addressed below.

9. Pyramid schemes attracted investors by offering high initial returns. Liabilities often exceeded assets, and ultimately the interest due to investors exceeded available funds. When investors attempted to withdraw their money, they learned that it no longer existed. By 1996, companies were voraciously competing for investors, and two companies attracted two million investors in a country of 3.5 million. Farmers sold off livestock and residents sold their homes to take part in the schemes, which promised in some cases to triple returns. By the beginning of 1997, companies stopped making interest payments, and by June, the national currency depreciated 40 percent to the U.S. dollar and prices inflated 28 percent from the beginning of the year.

10. This number is likely to be an underestimation of the total number of episodes due to the way full histories were collected. In addition, as shown by

Smith and Thomas (2003) for Malaysia, some of the shorter episodes far back in time are more likely to be underreported, particularly when the events are multiple and spanning a long period.

11. The number is obviously a gross underestimation of total migration, as it does not account for entire families that have moved abroad and, thus, are not in our sample.

12. This is not surprising given the composition of the split-off group being analyzed, which is entirely constituted by immediate household members. The behavior of other remitters may be rather different.

13. In index, computed using principal component analysis, is based on the household's ownership of eight durable goods in 1990.

14. It could also be a "temporal issue" in that the impact of current migration on current consumption is more direct postintegration.

15. Because of the low number of observations in the top rungs, we group the responses of the top four rungs.

16. In its third-level administrative subdivision, the country is divided into 309 communes (rural) and 65 municipalities (urban), for a total of 374 administrative units.

References

Barjaba, K. 2000. "Contemporary Patterns in Albanian Migration." *South-East Europe Review* 3(2): 57–64.

de Zwager, N., I. Gedeshi, E. Germenji, and C. Nikas. 2005. "Competing for Remittances." International Organization for Migration and government of Albania, Tirana. http://www.iomtirana.org.al/index.php/index.php?faqe=brochure.

Government of Albania. 2005. *National Strategy on Migration*. Tirana: Government of Albania and IOM.

Hahn, J., and J. Hausman. 2003. "Weak Instruments: Diagnosis and Cures in Empirical Economics." *American Economic Review* 93(2): 118–25.

Kilic, T., C. Carletto, B. Davis, and A. Zezza. 2009. "Investing Back Home: Return Migration and Business Ownership in Albania." *Economics of Transition* 17(3): 587–623.

King, R., and J. Vullnetari. 2003. "Migration and Development in Albania." Working Paper C5. Development Research Centre on Migration, Globalisation and Poverty, University of Sussex, Brighton.

McKenzie, D., and M. Sasin. 2007. "Migration, Remittances, Poverty, and Human Capital: Conceptual and Empirical Challenges." Policy Research Working Paper 4272. World Bank, Washington, DC.

Smith, J. P., and D. Thomas. 2003. "Remembrances of Things Past: Test-Retest Reliability of Retrospective Migration Histories." *Journal of the Royal Statistical Society: Series A (Statistics in Society)* 166(1): 23–49.

Staiger, D., and J. H. Stock. 1997. "Instrumental Variables Regression with Weak Instruments." *Econometrica* 65: 557–86.

World Bank. 2007. "Albania: Urban Growth, Migration and Poverty Reduction: A Poverty Assessment." PREM-ECA Region Report. World Bank, Washington, DC.

CHAPTER 5

Migration Choices, Inequality of Opportunities, and Poverty Reduction in Nicaragua[1]

Edmundo Murrugarra and Catalina Herrera

Introduction

Nicaragua is an illustrative case for analyzing the linkages between migration and poverty. With a per capita gross national income of US$1,000 in 2006 and a population of 5.2 million, it is the poorest country in the western hemisphere after Haiti. The poverty rate is 46 percent at the national level and almost twice as high in rural areas (World Bank 2008). Furthermore, Nicaragua is prone to natural disasters, adding an important component of economic and social vulnerability.

Migration and remittances play an increasing role in Nicaragua. According to the 2005 Living Standards Measurement Survey (LSMS), almost one-third of the Nicaraguan population was affected by migration or remittance flows, with about 14 percent of households reporting a migrant abroad and 22 percent receiving external remittances.[2] Remittances reached US$600 million in 2005, representing 40 percent of exports, 2.6 times foreign direct investment, and 12 percent of GDP (IMF 2006).

The main destinations for Nicaraguan migrants are Costa Rica and the United States, but the composition of migrants to these destinations has changed over time. Since 2000, a shift to Costa Rica away from the United States has consolidated a bipolar migration pattern: Nicaraguan migrants to Costa Rica are poorer, less educated, younger, and more likely to come from rural areas than those traveling to the United States. This is likely a reflection of the uneven distribution of social and economic opportunities such as access to education, social networks, and infrastructure.

Migration choices are household decisions based on the allocation of labor resources, made simultaneously with other labor supply, budget allocation, and human capital decisions. As discussed in McKenzie and Sasin (2007), establishing causality between migration and poverty (or other household outcomes) is difficult due to this joint decision-making process underlying different household outcomes. Poverty and migration linkages are also affected by the heterogeneity of migration choices, with different qualities of migration destinations involving intrinsically different costs and returns. Migration choices reflect the household's capacity to afford and benefit from those choices.

Using this conceptual framework, this chapter examines the determinants of Nicaraguan migration to the United States and Costa Rica and the poverty linkages of these different migration options to different socioeconomic groups. The next two sections discuss recent trends in migration and the bipolar nature of migration patterns. Next, the chapter combines information on migration and living conditions from the 2005 Nicaragua LSMS along with data on rainfall, migration networks, and location to instrument past migration choices in explaining consumption and poverty.

Recent Migration Trends in Nicaragua

The sluggish nature of economic growth in Nicaragua since 2000 is associated with natural disasters, reduced investment, a lagging agricultural sector, and adverse international prices. GDP growth in Nicaragua was about 4.4 percent during 1997–2001, and declined later to 3 percent due to poor performance in 2002 and 2003. This slowdown in growth is clearly observed in the agricultural sector, where one-fifth of Nicaragua's GDP is produced and 40 percent of the labor force is employed. Agricultural growth rates were halved from 5 percent to less than 2.4 percent between 1997–2001 and 2001–05, due largely to a number of droughts and the coffee price crisis in 2002.

Parallel to the economic slowdown, migration and remittances have increased their role in Nicaraguan social and economic dynamics. Around

10 percent of the population is living abroad—mostly in the United
States and Costa Rica—and official remittances have increased dramatically during the last ten years (Figure 5.1), passing US$600 million in
2005, equal to 12 percent of GDP.

The main destinations for Nicaraguan migrants are Costa Rica and
the United States, but the composition of these migration flows has
changed over time. Emigration to the United States was largely due to
the economic and political crisis during the 1980s, while migration to
Costa Rica is historically grounded in the early twentieth century, with
agricultural seasonal labor migration assisting in the Costa Rican
banana and coffee industries (Mahler 2006). Between 1979 and 1990,
about 60 percent of reported Nicaraguan migrants went to the United
States, according to the LSMS.[3] These earlier outflows are corroborated by evidence from the 2000 U.S. Census, which shows that 51
percent of Nicaraguan migrants into the United States arrived 25 years
earlier.[4]

The emigration pattern began to shift toward Costa Rica and away
from the United States in the 1990s, and this destination shift has accel-
erated with the recent increase in total migration flows (Figure 5.2).
Between 2001 and 2005, according to the LSMS data, the percentage
of households with a migrant abroad increased from 11 to 14 percent,
with 60 percent of migrants going to Costa Rica compared to only 30
percent to the United States, and the rest to other neighboring countries.[5] The survey evidence is corroborated by the 2005 Nicaragua
Census, which found that 48 percent of migrants left the country

Figure 5.1   Remittance Flows to Nicaragua, 1995–2005

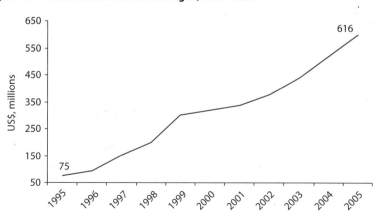

Source: World Bank, DECPG.

Figure 5.2   Nicaraguan Migrants to Costa Rica and the United States

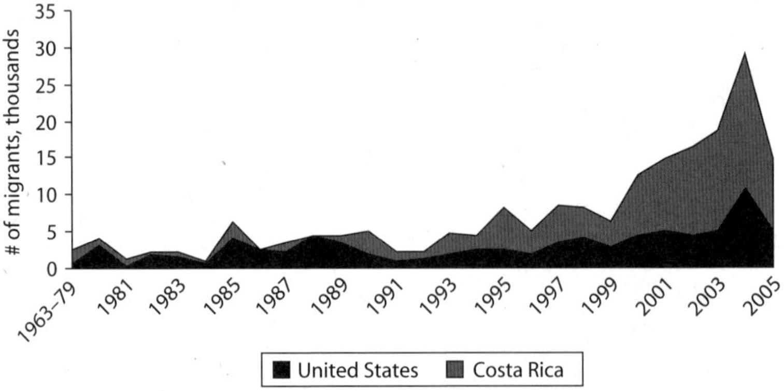

Source: LSMS 2005.

between 2000 and 2005, compared to only 22 percent between 1995 and 1999, and that 55 percent of migrants went to Costa Rica between 1995 and 2005, compared to 30 percent between 1985 and 1995 (INEC 2007).

According to the 2000 Costa Rica Census, more than 200,000 Nicaraguans were living in Costa Rica, but estimates based on Costa Rican birth records and fertility patterns suggest that the number is 283,000, or 6 percent of Costa Rica's population. While this shows the magnitude and relevance of the migration phenomenon for both countries, the impact could still be underestimated because the census does not capture seasonal Nicaraguan migration associated with peak harvest times in Costa Rica. Estimates of seasonal migrants could augment the original figure by 100,000.[6] The number of Nicaraguan household members absent during the year prior to the household survey is 60 percent higher than that of reported permanent migrants, suggesting that an important proportion of households are involved in seasonal migration.[7] Corroborative evidence of seasonal migration is also found in a survey of more than 4,000 households in northern provinces of Nicaragua, where half of the households are involved in seasonal migration (Macours and Vakis 2007).[8]

The substantial propensity for migration to Costa Rica is reflected in internal migration flows near the border. If migration to Costa Rica is increasing, it should be related to internal flows toward the border. According to the 2005 Nicaragua Census, 13 percent of Nicaraguans live in a department different from their birth place, and the departments having the largest proportion of residents not born in the place of census (besides the capital Managua) are Río San Juan and Región Autónoma del Atlántico Sur (RAAS) bordering Costa Rica. In fact, Río San Juan attracts populations from Chontales and RAAS, probably hiding transmigration patterns into Costa Rica. This chapter does not address internal mobility and its linkage to international migration, due to data limitations.

Bipolar Migration Patterns and Economic Opportunities

The recent shift of outflows to Costa Rica away from the United States has consolidated a differentiated migration profile between these two destination countries in which worse-off individuals go to Costa Rica and those who are better off migrate to the United States. Migration to the United States involves a larger financial cost of travel, additional cultural thresholds such as language, and more developed social networks to enhance employment opportunities. By contrast, migration to Costa Rica is cheaper, the destination is closer, the language is not problematic, and temporary or circular migration may reduce the burden of the integration process.

Migration choices thus reflect different socioeconomic backgrounds and the uneven distribution of social and economic opportunities, such as access to education, social networks, and infrastructure. A Nicaraguan migrant's average number of years of education is higher than the national average; however, this hides a distinction between those who migrate to Costa Rica, who on average have a primary education, and those moving to the United States, who generally have achieved additional years in secondary school (Table 5.1). The lower educational levels of Nicaraguan migrants in Costa Rica correspond to the reported activities they perform in the destination country. Migrants are concentrated in the northern provinces of Costa Rica, where agricultural work is predominant, and in the capital San José, where construction and housekeeping services are the core occupations. A recent assessment of poverty and living conditions in Costa Rica examined in detail the situation of the Nicaraguan migrants, showing their position in the bottom of the wage distribution and lower occupational status (World Bank 2007).

Nicaraguan emigration is predominantly an urban phenomenon but differs greatly between the United States and Costa Rica. Three out of four Nicaraguan migrants come from urban households, but this urban concentration is even more pronounced among migrants to the United States (92 percent).[9] Rural individuals account for more than 38 percent of those going to Costa Rica. If seasonal migration to Costa Rica associated

Table 5.1   Migrant Characteristics

	Total migrants	Costa Rica	United States	Other countries	Total population in Nicaragua
Actual age (mean)	32.5	29.4	36.9	31.3	—
Years of education	7.7	6.4	9.4	7.9	5.9[a]
Urban residence (%)	75.1	61.7	91.8	77.4	55.8
Region of origin (%)					
Managua	26.7	13.7	44.8	22.7	25.0
Pacifico	39.5	50.2	22.3	49.5	29.0
Central	25.2	23.6	28.2	22.5	32.0
Atlantico	8.7	12.5	4.7	5.4	14.0
Total	100.0	100.0	100.0	100.0	100.0

Source: LSMS 2005.
Note: — = not available
a. This average was calculated based on individuals who are 15 years old or older.

with the peak harvest times were better captured in census and survey instruments, this percentage would be significantly higher. By geographical location, most migrants to the United States are from Managua (45 percent), while those migrating to Costa Rica come from the Pacific region. While the Pacific region accounts for only 30 percent of the population, about half of the migration to Costa Rica is from this region.

Higher-income families are more likely to have a migrant abroad. Distinctive patterns of migration are observed across the income distribution, in terms of both propensity to migrate and choice of destination. This is immediately apparent when households with migrants are divided into consumption quintiles (Figure 5.3). Since consumption may be affected by migration and remittances, the distribution of migrants by household assets quintiles is also shown, corroborating the selective pattern of migration.[10]

The fact that poorer individuals are more likely to migrate to Costa Rica than to the United States can be confirmed by looking at destination choices by consumption quintile (Figure 5.4). The proportion of migrants to Costa Rica decreases as household per capita consumption increases. The percentage of migrants to Costa Rica in each quintile is larger than the percentage going to the United States, except for the highest quintile. While more than 80 percent of migrants from the poorest quintile go to Costa Rica, only one-fifth of those from the richest quintile choose that destination.

Moreover, 82 percent of the total volume of remittances is received by the top two quintiles. While in the lowest quintile a household receives on

Figure 5.3   Nicaragua Incidence of Migration by Quintile

Source: LSMS 2005.

Figure 5.4   Migrant Destination by Consumption Quintile

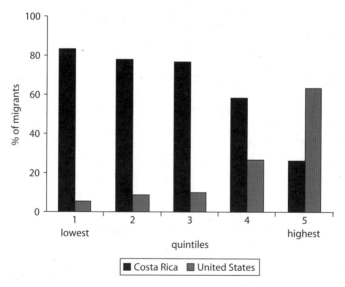

Source: LSMS 2005.

average US$332 per year, in the richest quintile a household receives approximately four times that amount. Remittances represent, on average, 2 percent of household consumption in the first quintile and 10 percent for those in the fifth quintile. In the case of seasonal migration, the average income brought home is around US$200 for selected communities in

Figure 5.5   Nicaragua Remittances Incidence by Quintile

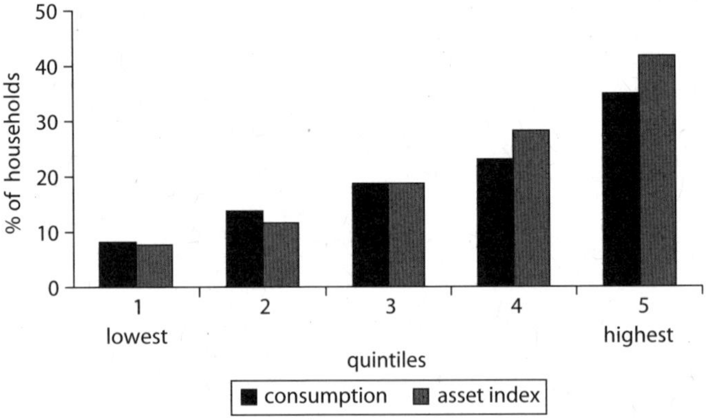

Source: LSMS 2005.

the north, representing close to 19 percent of total income (Macours and Vakis 2007).

Determinants of Migration Selectivity and Poverty Linkages

Since migration is a household response to economic prospects, including uncertainties caused by income or productivity shocks, the characteristics of migrants and their choice of destination will reflect differentiated opportunities to manage socioeconomic risks among Nicaraguan households. This section examines the differentiated patterns and impacts of migration destination together with individual, household, and community characteristics using a regression framework. We first model the decision to migrate and the choice of destination jointly in a multinomial choice setting where individuals can choose between not migrating at all and migrating to Costa Rica, to the United States, or to other countries.[11] The second stage of this analysis uses poverty equations, conditional on the migration decision, to explore if these differentiated migration patterns have distinct distributional impacts on household consumption levels and poverty.[12]

The analysis focuses on migration decisions during the 2002–05 period, using information from the 2005 LSMS. The analysis on migration decision uses characteristics such as educational attainment, age, and gender for individuals between ages 15 and 49. Household variables include demographic characteristics (size and composition); household head characteristics such as education, gender, and labor force participation; and the economic sector from which most incomes are drawn. Community characteristics include geographic attributes (urban/rural, department) and the existing migration network in the community (measured as the relative importance of the migrant to each destination in the corresponding *municipio*).

The results of this exercise show that migration choices between 2002 and 2005, when migration to Costa Rica was accelerating, were shaped by differences in household human and physical assets, and in migrants' ability to exploit existing social networks. Human and capital assets, geographic location, and access to social infrastructure each played a role in leading individuals to migrate, in general, and to migrate to specific destinations.

The results of the multinomial choice model corroborate that the drivers of migration to the United States and to Costa Rica are notably different. First, household reliance on agriculture increases the odds of migration, mainly to Costa Rica, suggesting that the lagging growth in agriculture has been an important push factor to Costa Rica. Geographical location of households can also determine the destination. Individuals in households in departments close to Managua—like Jinotega, Madriz, and Esteli—are more likely to migrate to the United States than those living far away from the capital. Individuals living in Río San Juan or RAAS, on the other hand, are more likely to go to Costa Rica, and the propensity to migrate to the United States is reduced drastically. Households with lower access to social infrastructure, as measured by the distance to the nearest health and education services, have lower propensities to migrate to Costa Rica, reflecting lower access to transport and communication services.[13]

Individual characteristics can also shape destination choices. An individual with primary schooling increases her or his odds of migrating to Costa Rica compared to not migrating at all by more than 50 percent, but higher levels of education do not increase these odds. On the other hand, higher levels of education increase the odds of migrating to the United States. These separating effects of education are confirmed in other studies that found increasing human capital beyond primary education reduces migration to Costa Rica compared to the United States (Vargas and Barquero 2005).

The impact of primary education is particularly important among females, whose odds of migrating to Costa Rica are increased threefold, while for males, primary education completion is not significant.[14] This evidence may also match the patterns of labor market absorption in Costa Rica, where females are predominantly absorbed into household services where some basic education may be required, while males are absorbed into agriculture and construction, where education may not be as important. The education level of the household head is also relevant: individuals in households where the head has a technical or tertiary education are only two-thirds as likely to migrate to Costa Rica compared to staying in Nicaragua.

Existing social networks of migrants in Costa Rica are playing an important role in the recent migration waves. Municipal migration networks for each destination are measured by the number of migrants to each destination who left Nicaragua before 2001 as a share of the total municipal population. These network variables are correlated with increased migration to Costa Rica, but not to the United States. One explanation for the differential impact of networks in destination choices is that for migration to the United States, direct family connections, educational attainment, and other skills are better instruments for insertion. On the other hand, social capital linkages and other informal mechanisms are exploited in migrating to and obtaining a job in Costa Rica. These linkages utilize community or municipal contacts beyond family connections to assess the prospects of finding jobs and gaining contact with future employers in Costa Rica. Employers, in turn, rely on these broader networks to access new labor given the recommendations of current workers (Borge 2005).

Social networks have a higher impact on migration probability to Costa Rica for the less skilled (Figure 5.6). The stronger effect of social networks for the less educated supports the findings of McKenzie and Rapoport (2006) in Mexico, where the role of networks decreases with education level of the community.

As an extension of this multinomial migration destination model, Murrugarra and Herrera (2008) analyze how extreme rainfall conditions (abnormally low or high) affected the recent migration flows away from the United States to Costa Rica as a result of household decisions to cope with income shocks.[15] The results indicate that the marginal impacts of the extreme weather conditions are likely to increase migration to Costa Rica, but not to the United States. The presence of a severe drought more than doubles the probability of migrating to Costa Rica compared to not moving, but does not affect the probability of migrating to the United States. On the other extreme, excess rainfall does not have a statistically significant impact on migrant destination choices.

Figure 5.6   Probability of Migration to Costa Rica, by Education Level

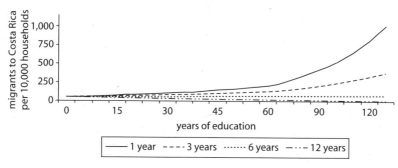

Source: LSMS 2005.

These results are consistent with the bipolar migration pattern found in Nicaragua since 2000, where severe droughts affect those involved in agriculture compared to better-off individuals, who have access to other instruments to cope with shocks. The Nicaraguan rural population, which predominantly goes to Costa Rica, is more vulnerable to extreme weather conditions, and droughts have become a push factor for labor mobility in the absence of other consumption or income-smoothing mechanisms.

A simple estimation of consumption levels indicates that the poverty rate in Nicaragua would have been 4 percentage points higher without remittances from migrants (Table 5.2). This effect is clearly observed in urban areas, where most migrants originate and where most remittances are sent. The effects are very important around the extreme poverty line: the extreme poverty rate would have been more than 18 percent (up from 14 percent) if remittances were not received in Nicaragua. This illustrates that while remittances to the poor are smaller, they still represent an important share of the budget, especially for extremely poor households.

These associated gains were also found after controlling for other socioeconomic factors, modeling either consumption or poverty indicators.[16] Two empirical strategies were employed. First, a probit model for the household poverty indicator was implemented to show the effect of having a migrant abroad. Controlling for demographic, socioeconomic, and geographic characteristics of the household, this marginal effect could potentially reduce the probability of being poor by 10.5 percentage points and increase household per capita consumption by 15 percent. Including the number of migrants as a variable—since almost one-third of Nicaraguan households with migrants have more than one migrant abroad (INEC 2006)—shows that the number of migrants is associated

Table 5.2   Poverty Rates with and without Remittances, 2005
percent

	(a) Total consumption	(b) Consumption without remmittances	(c) Difference (a)–(b)	(d) Std error (a)
General poverty				
National	46.0	49.7	–3.7	1.4
Urban	28.9	33.8	–4.9	1.8
Extreme poverty				
National	14.8	18.0	–3.2	0.8
Urban	5.4	9.1	–3.7	0.8
Rural	26.6	29.2	–2.6	1.4

Source: LSMS 2005.

Figure 5.7   Marginal Impacts on the Likelihood of Poverty by Migrant Destination

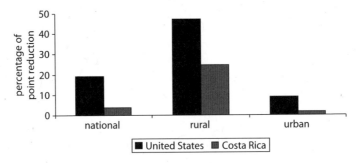

Source: LSMS 2005.
Note: The marginal impacts are calculated using a probit model. Results at national and rural level are at a 1% level of significance, while the urban areas are at a 10% level of significance.

with an 8 percent increase in consumption and a 7 percentage point reduction in poverty (Table 5A.2 in the annex).[17]

Second, the analysis distinguished migrants by country of destination. As expected, the marginal effect of migrating to the United States is significantly higher than the gains from migrating to Costa Rica (Figure 5.7 and table 5A.3 in the annex). Migration to the United States is associated with consumption gains at 17 percent and reductions in poverty to 17 percentage points at the national level. The associated gains for migration to Costa Rica are smaller but still show significant effects in rural areas, where households with migrants have an associated consumption gain of 11 percent and a reduction in the likelihood of poverty of 6 percentage points.

The observed gains from migration, however, may come with a direct cost on household well-being. Migration processes may affect household allocation of labor resources with different potential outcomes. Migration of adult males, for example, could represent an increased need for labor from other members (females or older children), especially if households are involved in self-employment or other household-based productive activities. This could, in turn, lead to a decline in schooling among older children or less time by other members spent with the children.

The additional income can offset some of these negative effects. Arends-Kuening and Duryea (2006) find in Nicaragua that adolescents between 14 and 16 years old living in a single-parent household experience a decline in school enrollment from 67 to 55 percent, after accounting for other income losses. Cox-Edwards and Ureta (2003), on the other hand, found that migration and associated remittances had a positive effect on school retention. In a survey of poor Nicaraguan villages in the north, Macours and Vakis (2007) found that children of seasonal migrant mothers fare slightly worse with regard to development indicators (cognitive and health status) compared to nonmigrants. These outcomes, however, are attributed to other social and economic characteristics of the household and communities, and not to migration itself. Accounting for other factors, children from seasonal migrants show better cognitive achievement outcomes, underscoring the important role of extended family networks in providing care for young children and the empowerment of women due to migration.

Conclusion and Policy Implications

Migration and remittances have an increasing role in the social and economic dynamics of Nicaragua, where almost one-third of households either have a migrant or receive remittances from abroad. Increasing migration outflows to Costa Rica in recent years have defined a distinctive migration profile. Nicaraguan migrants to Costa Rica are poorer, less educated, younger, and more likely to come from rural areas than their counterparts going to the United States. Scarce opportunities in rural areas, living in departments neighboring Costa Rica, and access to roads and other social infrastructure facilitate migration flows to Costa Rica, which attracted 60 percent of Nicaraguan emigrants between 2001 and 2005. The migration to Costa Rica is primarily by working-age individuals who find work in agriculture, construction, and household services, sectors that require little human capital. Basic levels of education increase the chances of choosing Costa Rica as destination, while higher levels of education increase the odds of migrating to the United States.

The associated gains from migration and remittances have reduced the Nicaraguan poverty level by 4 to 5 percentage points, with a more important impact for the extreme poor. Most of the benefits are associated with migration to the United States, while the benefits from migrating to Costa Rica seem more modest and concentrated in rural areas. Still, those smaller benefits play an important role for the sending households. Moreover, considering the frequency of natural disasters such as drought, migration to Costa Rica is a key coping mechanism for rural households that do not have other instruments to manage their socioeconomic risks. Although migration and remittances generate household consumption gains, they may also come with costs that need to be examined in detail— for example, the impact on education and labor patterns of household members who do not emigrate.

Since destinations are driven by socioeconomic characteristics and the returns from migration heavily depend on destination choice, public policy design should incorporate distinct mechanisms according to destination to enhance the benefits of migration and manage the risks. Migration to the United States calls for an agenda focused on the facilitation of remittances, the more tangible benefits from migration.

The lower returns from Costa Rican migration—which is more common for poorer, younger, and less educated migrants—raise a number of policy issues that address the specificities of South-South migration. First, this migration is more likely to be undocumented, which in turn can affect the labor market outcomes of immigrants. Bilateral agreements need to be developed to protect migrants' rights and to ensure the portability of some social security benefits. The recent increase in migration to Costa Rica provides an opportunity to establish a dialogue on bilateral agreements that provide temporary migrants a safer and more protected migration environment (Borge 2006).[18]

Second, programs to benefit the poor may see their objective offset by household responses to policies. For example, it has been documented that public transfers could displace between 30 and 40 percent of private transfers, such as remittances. If that is the case and remittances play an important role in the incomes of the poor, social transfers need to be designed to minimize these displacement effects and seek complementarities between public and private resources. The challenge is to create complementarities without generating additional incentives for migration. For example, establishing home-town associations linking diaspora communities to particular sending areas fosters synergies between the public interventions and private initiatives. For example, Mexico has implemented schemes such as *Iniciativa Ciudadana 3 por 1*, where every dollar remitted by the home-town associations is matched with one dollar each from the federal, state, and municipal governments. One essential aspect of designing and implementing these policies is to strengthen the monitoring and evaluation systems on migration and remittances, mainly though improving the data collection.

Annex

Conceptual Framework of the Migration Choice Model

The decision to migrate and the choice of destination are modeled jointly in a multinomial choice setting where individuals can choose between not moving, migrating to Costa Rica (low-return destination), and migrating to the United States (high costs, higher returns).[19] Following other models of selectivity (Chiquiar and Hanson 2005; McKenzie and Rapoport 2006), labor income depends on the returns to schooling in each location:

$$\text{Home: } \ln w_0 = \mu_0 + \delta_0 S$$
$$\text{Destination 1 (High): } \ln w_1 = \mu_1 + \delta_1 S$$
$$\text{Destination 2 (Low): } \ln w_2 = \mu_2 + \delta_2 S$$

where w_i is the wage in location i, and S is the schooling level of the individual. Attaining those wages involves some costs for those planning to migrate. Usually the cost of migration reflects the prevailing "migration technology" and includes factors such as distance, networks, and other proxies for costs. Here, migration costs are specified as:

$$\text{Destination 1 (High): } C_1 = C_1(n_1)$$
$$\text{Destination 2 (Low): } C_2 = C_2(n_2)$$

where n_i is the migration network for destination i, preferably a measure of network at the local level, suggesting the social network accessible to the individual. The decision to migrate to destination 1 will be taken if the net benefits (NB) are higher than other options:

$$NB_1 > NB_0: \ln w_1 - \ln (w_0 + C_1) > 0$$
$$NB_1 > NB_2: \ln (w_1 - C_1) - \ln (w_2 - C_2) > 0$$

This can be better observed in Figure 5A.1, a standard graph in previous models of selectivity with one destination. In those models, individuals with schooling level between M_0 and M_1 have the incentive to migrate. Individuals with very low schooling would face large costs for either destination, and returns will not compensate. Similarly, individuals with very high educational attainment could afford the trip but the returns, compared to those in their home country, do not compensate for the effort.[20]

In our case, the model with two destinations allows for the possibility of differentiated migration patterns across schooling levels. Figure 5A.2

Figure 5A.1   Migration Decision (One Destination)

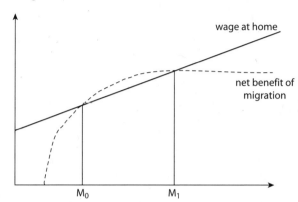

Figure 5A.2   Migration Decision (Two Destinations)

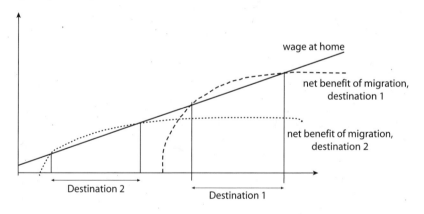

shows a case where individuals with higher schooling levels choose destination 1, since it provides larger gains for that specific schooling group. This would be the case for secondary graduates who go to the United States. Individuals with lower levels of schooling (some primary education) prefer destination 2. These two groups are completely separated in the specification, but in reality they may not be fully distinguished.

Table 5A.1   Results for the Multinomial Logit by Destination

Variables	Costa Rica Coefficient	Std error	United States Coefficient	Std error
A. Individual characteristics				
Gender	0.150	0.165	.841**	0.285
Age	−0.060	0.012	−.0325**	0.013
School completion				
Primary	0.467**	0.236	1.469	1.175
Secondary	0.543*	0.308	1.315	1.138
Technical	1.48*	0.464	2.017	1.320
Terciary	0.87**	0.477	1.753	1.177
Household size (logarithm)	−2.302*	0.282	−2.523***	0.409
Share of babies in household	4.741*	0.833	4.044***	1.061
Share of kids in household	4.886*	0.615	3.777***	0.702
Share of seniors in household	1.875*	1.123	−0.828	1.465
Share of adults in household (omitted)				
B. Household head's characteristics				
Is female	−0.491*	0.283	0.266	0.354
Is single or divorced	0.504*	0.268	0.226	0.338
Age	0.289*	0.057	0.087	0.068
Age*age	−.0023***	0.001	0.000	0.001
Feels indigenous	0.857	0.575	−0.955	0.921
Has a job	0.302	0.396	−0.704	1.237
Works in blue collar	−0.217	0.349	1.056	1.119
Is self-employed	−0.294	0.460	2.133	1.137
Works as an entrepreneur or chief	−0.269	0.265	1.009*	1.135
Works in industry	0.090	0.323	−1.477	0.816
Works in services	−0.417	0.707	−0.819	1.088
Works in construction	0.138	0.465	−0.438	0.821
Works in commerce	−0.079	0.321	−0.090	0.461
Works in financial services	−31.559***	0.335	−0.987	0.704
Works in other services	−0.590	0.380	−0.992*	0.595
Works in agriculture (omitted)				
Head's school completion				
Primary	−0.212	0.192	0.515	0.451
Secondary	−0.208	0.305	1.263**	0.468
Technical	−1.360*	0.765	−0.606	0.847
Terciary	−0.944	0.770	0.932	0.708
C. Household characteristics				
Urban	−0.103	0.226	0.579	0.493
Index of communication goods 2001	−0.134	0.110	−0.153	0.101
Index of durables goods 2001	0.012	0.079	0.076	0.054
Index of access to road	0.056	0.115	−0.170	0.316
Index of state of the roads	0.032	0.167	0.208	0.406

(continued)

Table 5A.1 Results for the Multinomial Logit by Destination *(continued)*

	Costa Rica		United States	
Variables	Coefficient	Std error	Coefficient	Std error
Has telephone service	−0.023	0.105	−0.0562***	0.104
Index of dwelling conditions	0.009	0.071	−0.382*	0.175
Index of distance of social services	−0.2815***	0.089	−0.207	0.213
D. Community characteristics				
Departments				
Nueva segovia	0.171	0.542	0.810	0.548
Jinotega	0.004	0.529	1.581**	0.671
Madriz	0.225	0.497	1.371**	0.495
Esteli	0.578	0.440	1.990***	0.491
Chinandega	0.582	0.426	1.027**	0.483
Leon	1.002**	0.407	−0.243	0.642
Matagalpa	0.079	0.500	0.092	0.465
Boaca	−0.071	0.501	1.353***	0.419
Masaya	−0.124	0.502	−0.241	0.690
Chontales	0.829**	0.437	−1.960*	1.056
Granada	0.705	0.468	−0.442	0.690
Carazo	0.884*	0.486	−1.108	0.853
Rivas	0.170	0.492	−28.289*	0.971
Rio san Juan	1.224*	0.419	−29.796*	0.663
Raan	2.575*	1.169	1.096*	0.653
Raas	.934*	0.425	−0.264	1.288
Index of social networks, Costa Rica	12.401***	3.428	−41.715**	12.965
Index of social networks, United States	−14.993	9.894	−3.096	9.690
Index of social networks, other countries	−6.261	16.533	54.057***	11.857
Constant	−9.196***	1.471	−7.045***	2.181

Note: Number of observations (Individuals between 14–46): 2,440,752. Significance level: * = 10%; ** = 5%; *** = 1%.

Table 5A.2 Marginal Impact of Migration on Consumption and Poverty
percent

	Consumption	Poverty reduction
Household with migrant		
Total	14.9***	10.4***
Urban	14.3***	5.17*
Rural	13.8***	14.6***
Number of migrants		
Total	8.2***	6.8***
Urban	8.5***	3.9**
Rural	5.9***	6.3***

Source: LSMS 2005.
Note: Significance level: * = 10%; ** = 5; *** = 1%.

Table 5A.3   Impact of Migration on Consumption and Poverty by Destination
percent

	National	Urban	Rural
Consumption model (% gains)			
Household has migrant			
United States	31.0***	26.8***	41.1***
Costa Rica	5.0	2.1	11.5***
Number of migrants			
United States	17.2***	15.9***	13.1**
Costa Rica	2.4	0.1	6.1**
Poverty model (point reduction)			
Household has migrant			
United States	19.2***	8.9**	47.1***
Costa Rica	3.8	1.8	24.5**
Number of migrants			
United States	17.2***	10.5***	14.9
Costa Rica	4.0*	−0.2	6.3***

Source: LSMS 2005 and World Bank estimates.
Note: Significance level: * = 10%; ** = 5%; *** = 1%.

Notes

1. This chapter was produced under the activities of the World Bank Nicaragua Poverty Assessment, and under the migration program of PRMPR department of the World Bank. We thank earlier conversations with Diego Angel-Urdinola, Florencia Castro-Leal, David McKenzie, participants at the Poverty Workshop in Managua and at the World Bank Economists Forums of 2007 and 2008. Special thanks to the staff from the Instituto Nacional de Estadísticas y Censos (INEC) for helping to improve our understanding of the Nicaraguan socioeconomic context and the methodological and data issues. This paper does not represent the views of the World Bank or its member countries. Both authors are with the World Bank, Poverty Reduction Unit. Corresponding author: E. Murrugarra (emurrugarra@worldbank.org).

2. Remittances are defined as workers' remittances, compensation of employees, and migrant transfers.

3. The LSMS does not capture entire migrating households as migrants, so the total number of migrants could differ from other sources, such as the Nicaragua Census. This measurement issue is discussed for the Mexican case by McKenzie (2006).

4. The data were extracted from the 1 percent sample of the 2000 U.S. Census. A migrant is defined as a person who was born outside the United States.

Accordingly, there were 234,328 Nicaraguan migrants in the United States in 2000, which represents 4.5 percent of the current Nicaraguan population.

5. Guatemala, El Salvador, Honduras, Mexico, and Panama.

6. There is no information in the 2005 LSMS about seasonal migration. The number of household members who were absent less than nine months, which could serve as a proxy, represents 7 percent of the population.

7. The survey, however, does not include information on the purpose of these absences or the destination.

8. CEPAL (2007) has estimated that irregular migration could be of equal size to that of the migrant population captured by the Costa Rican Census in 2000.

9. This predominantly urban feature is different from the characterization found in other Central American countries, where most migrants are from rural areas (CEPAL 2006). This may be due to the fact that the 2005 LSMS does not provide information on seasonal migrants, who are more likely to come from rural settings.

10. Clearly there is a reverse causality and endogeneity problem here. It may be the case that the higher wealth status of migrants can be the result of migration rather than the other way around, or that some unobserved factors (such as entrepreneurship) influence both wealth status and migration propensity. Assets owned in a household reflect long-term welfare status and thus are less likely to be affected by migrants' departures. In the empirical analysis of conditional distributions, migration decisions are conditioned on household assets owned before the migrant's departure. The asset index was constructed by the principal components method and includes variables about the dwelling conditions (owning, material of roof, floor, access to water, etc.) and possession of different housing assets (TV, radio, microwave, motorcycle, bicycle, etc.).

11. The exclusion of migration to other countries as a choice does not affect the results of the analysis.

12. A more detailed explanation of the conceptual framework is found in the Annex, where the complete results of the multinomial choice model under different specifications are presented in Table 5A.1.

13. This assumes that access to social services can proxy access to transportation networks, which is plausible because this distance was measured by a compound index of the distance and time from the household to the closest school and medical center.

14. These results are obtained by estimating the multinomial logit for male and female individuals separately.

15. The role of natural disasters is shaping migration flows. This was recognized in 1998, when Costa Rica granted legal status to 152,000 immigrants after Hurricane Mitch hit Nicaragua (Bail 2007). Baez and Santos (2006), using the

1999 Nicaragua LSMS, estimated that around 17 percent of households migrated permanently due to Hurricane Mitch. Central America, and Nicaragua in particular, is a region prone to natural disasters, adding an important vulnerability to the economic and social context. During 1970–99 Nicaragua experienced by far the highest losses in the Latin American region as a percentage of GDP due to natural disasters.

16. Decisions on migration, remittances, labor supply, expenditure allocation, school attendance, child labor, and so on are usually made simultaneously. Hence characteristics which explain migration and remittances may also shape household expenditure patterns. Moreover, many of the characteristics that influence these decisions are unobservable. These issues make it difficult to establish causality and bias the typical reduced-form regression framework. McKenzie and See Sasin (2007).

17. The consumption equation was also estimated using dummy variables for zero, one, two, three, or more migrants at the household level. A detailed analysis distinguishing the number of migrants in each household shows that the associated gains in consumption are revealed for urban households with two or more migrants, while among rural households additional migrants beyond the first contribute only marginally.

18. Spain is an example of a country with active bilateral agreement policies with sending countries like Morocco, Colombia, Ecuador, and Romania. The objective is to manage the market for immigrant labor and ensure basic labor conditions, thus improving the benefits of migration.

19. The exclusion of migration to other countries as a choice does not affect the results of the analysis.

20. In selectivity models, this is used to show how changes in the cost of migration will affect the skill profile of migrants. For example, cheaper migration costs due to increased networks will shift the net benefit curve upward, allowing new migrants. The final composition of new migrants will depend on the relative magnitudes of newly entering migrants from below M_0 and above M_1.

References

Adams, R. 2004. "Remittances and Poverty in Guatemala." DECRG, World Bank, Washington, DC.

Baez, J., and I. Santos. 2006 "Children's Vulnerability to Shocks: Hurricane Mitch in Nicaragua as a Natural Experiment." Working Paper. Syracuse University.

Bail, R. 2007. "Nicaragua Exports Its Poor." *Le Monde Diplomatique*, January 2007. http://mondediplo.com/2007/01/12nicaragua.

Banerjee, A., and E. Duflo. 2007. "The Economic Lives of the Poor." *Journal of Economic Perspectives* 21(1): 141–67.

Baumistier, E. 2006. "Migración Internacional y Desarrollo en Nicaragua." Serie Población y Desarrollo no. 67. CEPAL.

Borge, D. 2005. "La Fuerza de Los Vínculos Débiles en la Inserción Laboral de Los Migrantes Nicaragüenses." *Población y Salud en Mesoamérica* 3(1), July/December.

———. 2006. "Migración y Políticas Públicas: Elementos a Considerar para la Administración de la Migraciones entre Nicaragua y Costa Rica." *Población y Salud en Mesoamérica* 3(2), January.

Damm, Anna. 2009. "Determinants of Recent Immigrants' Location Choices: Quasi Experimental Evidence." *Journal of Population Economics* 22(1): 145–74.

de la Briere, B., E. Sadoulet, A. de Janvry, and S. Lambert. 2002. "The Roles of Destination, Gender, and Household Composition in Explaining Remittances: An Analysis for the Dominican Sierra." *Journal of Development Economics* 68: 309–28.

Economist Intelligence Unit. 2006. "Country Profile: Nicaragua 2006."

Fafchamps, M., and F. Gubert. 2007. "Risk Sharing and Network Formation." *American Economic Review Papers and Proceedings* 97(2): 75–79.

Filmer, D., and L. Pritchett. 1998. "Estimating Wealth Effects without Expenditure Data or Tears: An Application to Educational Enrollments in States of India." World Bank, Washington, DC.

Gonzalez, M., and E. Lizano. 2006. "Bancarizacion de las Remesas de Inmigrantes Nicarguenses en Costa Rica." Series de trabajos ocasionales del FOMIN—BID.

International Monetary Fund. 2006. "Nicaragua." Country Report No. 06/174. IMF, Washington, DC.

Macours, K., and R. Vakis. 2007. "Seasonal Migration and Early Childhood Development." World Bank, Washington, DC.

McKenzie, D., and H. Rapoport. 2006. "Self Selection Patterns in Mexico-US Migration: The Role of Migrant Networks." DECRG, World Bank, Washington, DC.

McKenzie, D., and M. Sasin. 2007. "Migration, Remittances and Human Capital: Conceptual and Empirical Challenges." Policy Research Working Paper 4272, World Bank, Washington, DC.

Mahler, S. 2006. "Central America: Crossroads of the Americas." *Migration Information Source*, April.

Marquette, C. 2006. "Nicaraguan Migrants and Poverty in Costa Rica." Centro Centroamericano de Poblacion, Universidad de Costa Rica.

Vargas, J., and J. Barquero. 2005. "Capital Humano y Social de los Nicaragüense con Experiencia Migratoria a Costa Rica y Estados Unidos." *Estudios Migratorios Latinoamericanos* 19(56).

World Bank. 2003. "Nicaragua Poverty Assessment: Raising Welfare and Reducing Vulnerability." Report No. 26128-NI. World Bank, Washington, DC.

———. 2007. "Costa Rica Poverty Assessment: Recapturing Momentum for Poverty Reduction." Report No. 35910-CR. World Bank, Washington, DC.

CHAPTER 6

How Can Developing Country Governments Facilitate International Migration for Poverty Reduction?

John Gibson and David McKenzie

Introduction

The massive differences in income across countries allow individuals and households to escape from poverty through international migration. For example, McKenzie, Gibson, and Stillman (2008) find Tongans who migrate to New Zealand under a visa lottery-type program experience a 263 percent increase in income within the first year of migrating. Under more heroic assumptions, Clemens and Pritchett (2008) illustrate that migration is a route out of poverty for individuals from a wide range of countries—for example, they estimate that four out of every five Haitians who have reached an income of US$10 per day did so by moving to the United States. However, as of 2005, only three percent of the world's population lived outside of their country of birth.[1] The puzzle then is why more people do not escape poverty by migrating to another country, while the challenge for policy makers in the developing world is determining whether there are policies they can pursue to make it easier for their citizens to escape poverty through migration.

One possible explanation for why more of the poor don't migrate is that they don't want to. In seven nationally representative surveys taken in 2005 and 2006, respondents aged 15 and over were asked whether they would like to work abroad if they could do so legally. Figure 6.1 reports the results for individuals coming from the poorest 25 percent of households in each country. In the wealthier countries of Malaysia and Romania, it is indeed the case that the majority of those who are poor do not wish to migrate. However, in poorer countries we see many poor individuals expressing a desire to migrate, with most preferring temporary to permanent migration. While one should always be cautious in interpreting these hypothetical questions, the large difference in magnitude between the number of poor expressing a desire to work abroad and the number actually doing so strongly suggests that there are a large number of poor people in the world who would like to try and escape poverty through international migration that are currently not able to do so.

The main reasons that more of the poor don't escape poverty through migration are high costs and few opportunities.[2] This chapter draws on work we have done in Mexico, the Pacific, and worldwide to provide

Figure 6.1   Many of the Poor Do Want to Migrate, But Only Temporarily

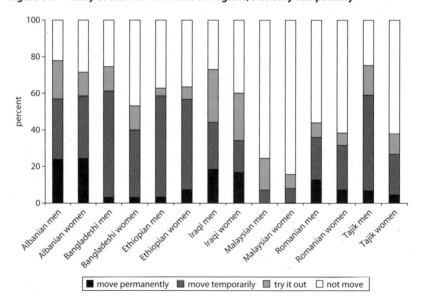

Source: Authors' own analysis from Intermedia/World Bank nationally representative surveys, 2005–06. Figures shown are responses for approximately the bottom quartile in each country. See World Bank (2006b) for additional description of the data.

some concrete examples of policies developing countries can pursue to increase the poverty-reducing impact of international migration by lowering costs and expanding opportunities.[3] The main policies discussed are:

- Removing barriers that developing countries put in place to prevent their citizens from emigrating. These include high prices and cumbersome procedures for passports and legal restrictions on the emigration of women.
- Increasing the poverty-reducing benefits of remittances from migrants by lowering remittance costs.
- Actively engaging in bilateral migration agreements to expand the opportunities for the poor to migrate. A good example is the new seasonal worker program that allows Pacific Islanders to work in New Zealand.

There are of course other examples of active policies that developing governments can put in place to reduce the costs and broaden the range of opportunities for international migration available to the poor on which this chapter does not focus. The most famous example is that of the Philippines, which has a very proactive approach to emigration. This includes licensing recruitment agencies, marketing its workers worldwide, signing 56 bilateral treaties with receiving countries, and providing pre-departure orientation seminars to potential migrants. While the basic features of this system are relatively well known (see IOM 2005; Wehrfritz and Vitug 2005) and have been copied in part by several other countries, there does not appear to be any serious economic analysis of the impact of such a system on poverty levels in the Philippines. In part this is because the system has been in place for so long, making before-after comparisons difficult with available data. The new seasonal worker program we study contains some features similar to the Philippines model and, in time, will allow estimation of the poverty-reducing impact of such policies.

The remainder of the chapter is structured as follows. The second part uses the example of Mexico to show how lowering the costs of migration makes migration increasingly pro-poor. The third part then shows how some of these costs are imposed by developing countries and how removing them can increase migration. The fourth section discusses how lowering remittance costs can increase remittance income received by remaining household members, and the fifth section shows how a temporary migration program can expand opportunities for the poor to migrate. The sixth part concludes the chapter.

Lowering Costs Increases the Ability of the Poor to Migrate

Sjaastad's (1962) classic economic model of migration views migration as an investment, requiring individuals to incur the costs of moving to generate the return from higher incomes. Migration is often a decision of the family, not just of an individual, particularly in developing countries, where imperfect credit and insurance markets create a rationale for migrating to diversify risk and finance costly household investment activities (Stark and Levhari 1982; Stark and Bloom 1985). However, it is precisely these imperfect credit markets that limit the ability of poor households to finance the costs of international migration.

One way poor households are able to overcome the high costs of migration is through the use of migration networks. Networks of migrants from the same community can use the income gained abroad to provide loans to new migrants, allowing them to overcome liquidity constraints that prevent migration. The network can also act to lower the psychic and financial costs of migrating for other community members, such as by providing assistance and housing in the first few days of arrival, and as in cases such as Mexican migration, lowering the costs of *coyotes* (smugglers) and assisting in crossing borders illegally (Espinosa and Massey 1997; Dolfin and Genicot 2006).[4] In McKenzie and Rapoport (2007), we show that as the network size grows, the migration pattern from communities in Mexico switches from being one in which only the relatively well-off migrate to the United States to one in which the poor are more likely to migrate than are the rich.

Figure 6.2 extends the analysis of McKenzie and Rapoport (2007) to show how the likelihood of a male household head migrating to the United States varies with the size of the migration network in his community, a proxy for migration costs.[5] When the network is small, with less than 5 percent of the adults in the community ever having migrated, almost no males living in households below the $1 per person per day poverty line migrate, and migrants tend to be drawn from the upper-middle of the expenditure distribution in a community.[6] As the network grows, the likelihood of migration grows for all wealth groups, but increases more for the poor. As a result, in communities where 20 percent or more of the community members have ever migrated, migration is heavily concentrated among those living on less than $2 per person per day, and the likelihood of migration is greatest for the very poor. This demonstrates that reducing costs allows the poor to increasingly become involved in international migration.

Figure 6.2   Migration Becomes More Pro-Poor as the Cost of Migrating Falls

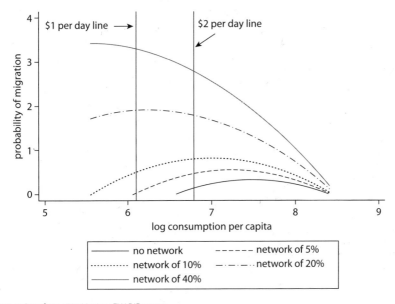

Source: Data from 1997 Mexican ENADID survey.

Note: Lines are fitted coefficients from modifying the instrumental variables regression in column 2, Table 3 of McKenzie and Rapoport (2007), to use log consumption per capita instead of log consumption as the regressor of interest. Network size measures the percentage of adults aged 15 and over in the community who have ever migrated.

Some of These Costs Are Barriers Developing Countries Put in the Way of Their Own Citizens

Lowering the costs of migration therefore allows the poor greater opportunity to participate in international migration and use migration as a means of leaving poverty. The previous section showed one way that costs can fall, through the development of community networks. What can policy makers do to lower the costs individuals face in migration? The first thing they can do is to not put large expenses in the way of their own citizens who wish to emigrate.

One form of these expenses is the monetary and time costs associated with obtaining a passport, the most basic document needed for legal travel abroad. Data on the cost of a passport were collected for 127 countries in October 2005.[7] There is remarkable variation in the cost of a passport across different countries, with the cost of a five-year passport having a median price of US$39, but varying from free in Armenia to US$333 in Turkey. High passport prices are particularly a barrier to migration for the poor, so we standardize passport costs by per capita GDP for comparison purposes. There are 14 countries where a passport costs more than 10 percent of per capita income, topped by the Democratic Republic of Congo, where a passport is 125 percent of per capita income. Eleven of these countries are in Africa. However, other African countries such as Swaziland, Kenya, Ghana, and Botswana charge less than US$6 for a passport.

After controlling for the income level of a country, high passport costs relative to GDP are found in countries with poor regulatory quality, low government effectiveness, and higher levels of corruption (McKenzie 2007). In contrast, there is no significant association between the rate of high-skilled emigration rate from a country and passport costs, suggesting that passport prices are not being set by countries to extract rents from the rich, and that richer, more-skilled migration is not affected by the cost of a passport.

Higher passport costs per capita are associated with lower migration rates. Figure 6.3 illustrates this by showing the passport cost per capita and emigration rate per capita for developing countries with the highest and lowest passport costs per capita. This negative association continues to hold in a regression context, controlling for income per capita, population,

Figure 6.3   High Passport Costs Are Associated with Lower Migration Rates

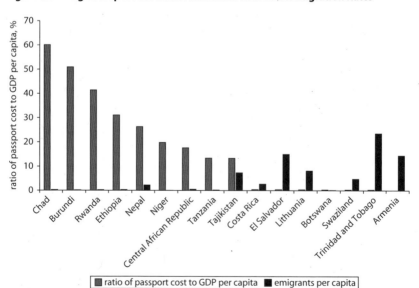

ratio of passport cost to GDP per capita   ■ emigrants per capita

Source: Data from McKenzie (2007).

and governance. In particular, regression results show that lowering passport costs by one percentage point is associated with a 0.75 percentage point increase in emigrants per capita (McKenzie 2007).

In addition to the financial costs involved in obtaining a passport, there are also noticeable differences in the administrative barriers countries put in the way of citizens seeking to obtain a passport. These include whether or not passports can be obtained by mail or only in person, and how decentralized passport offices are. In some countries, such as Nepal, until recently, anyone who wanted a passport had to travel to the capital city to obtain it. The time taken to get the passport also ranges a lot across countries, from 45 minutes in El Salvador to 5 weeks in India and 6 weeks in South Africa. Long waits act as an additional barrier to quickly obtaining documentation and leaving when a job opportunity presents itself, and may give rise to corruption with officials accepting bribes in exchange for faster processing. For example, witnesses in a parliamentary hearing in Namibia testified that many of the passport-issuing officials would frequently close their offices for personal business, leading to months-long waits for passports and bribes of four times the cost of a passport for faster service (Philander 2005).

High passport costs and burdensome procedures are an implicit barrier that many developing countries place in the way of their citizens who wish to emigrate. However, a handful of countries also have in place more explicit barriers that affect the migration possibilities of certain groups, especially women. Table 6.1 details the countries that place restrictions on the rights of certain groups of citizens to travel abroad. Panel A shows countries with legal restrictions on the ability of women to travel or obtain a passport. These restrictions usually take the form of preventing unmarried women traveling without the permission of their father or adult relative, and of married women traveling without the permission of their husband. These restrictions are significantly associated with less migration from a country: countries that restrict the rights of women to migrate have 5 to 6 percent fewer migrants per capita than countries with similar income, population, and governance levels without these restrictions (McKenzie 2007). The other types of common legal barriers are restrictions on travel of citizens of national service age (Panel B), and restrictions on the rights of all citizens to travel (Panel C). These restrictions require citizens to obtain government permission or an exit visa in order to travel. While permission may be granted in most cases in some of these countries, the process of requiring this permission introduces additional costs and uncertainty into the migration decision. Poor data quality from many of these countries prevents econometric analysis of

Table 6.1   Legal Restrictions That Countries Place on Travel of Their Own Citizens

A. Countries with travel restrictions on women

Afghanistan	Kuwait
Congo, Dem. Rep.	Myanmar
Egypt, Arab Rep.	Qatar (if under 30)
(if unmarried and under 21)	Saudi Arabia
Gabon	Sudan
Iran, Islamic Rep.	Syrian Arab Republic
	Uganda
	United Arab Emirates

B: Countries with travel restrictions on citizens of national service age

Algeria	Israel
Armenia	Kazakhstan
Azerbaijan	Lebanon
Egypt, Arab Rep.	Singapore

C: Countries where government permission or an exit visa is needed for travel

Armenia	Iran, Islamic Rep.	Tajikistan
Belarus	Iraq	Ukraine
Cuba	Myanmar	Uzbekistan
Eritrea	Korea, Dem. People's Rep.	Yemen, Rep.
	Saudi Arabia	
	Sudan	

Source: Country reports of U.S. Department of State (2007).

the strength of association between these barriers and emigration rates from these countries. Nevertheless, it is hard to believe that the general restrictions on travel practiced in the countries in Panel C do not negatively affect the ability of citizens from these countries to take advantage of migration opportunities abroad.

The existence of these barriers shows that there is policy latitude on the part of many developing countries to enhance the ability of their citizens to emigrate. Reduction of the cost of a passport, faster processing times, and the removal of any legal restrictions on emigration offer the potential for reaping additional gains from migration. It seems likely that such restrictions are more likely to bind poor emigrants than richer, so that removing them will enhance the opportunities for poorer individuals to migrate.

Lower Remittance Costs to Increase Remittances from Existing Migrants

A second area where government policy can increase the poverty-reducing benefits of migration is by lowering the costs of sending remittances. Remittances are one of the most direct ways that the migration of an individual can lower poverty for household members and other relatives remaining in the sending country. Lowering the cost of sending these remittances has become one of the most discussed areas for policy intervention in recent years (see World Bank 2006a), in part because doing so is viewed as politically uncontroversial compared to efforts to increase the opportunities for migration. A variety of policies has been proposed for lowering these costs, including increasing competition in the remittance market, improving the transparency of fees, removing burdensome regulations on money transfer, and expanding migrants' access to banking services.

The typical cost of sending a remittance consists of two components: a fixed fee and an exchange rate commission.[8] A lump-sum fixed fee means that the effective cost of sending a remittance falls as the amount sent increases. For example, Western Union charges a fixed fee of NZ$20 along with a 6 percent exchange rate commission in sending money from New Zealand to Tonga.[9] The effective cost of sending NZ$50 is thus 32.9 percent, which drops to 21.8 percent for NZ$100, 14.6 percent for NZ$200, and 7.9 percent for NZ$1,000. To the extent that poorer households are the potential recipients of smaller remittance transactions, high costs of sending money will be of much greater importance to them than to richer households.[10]

However, the extent to which policies to reduce remittance costs will lower poverty depend crucially on who benefits from lower-cost remittance systems. There are two aspects of this. The first is whether any additional savings from lower transactions costs are passed on to the remittance receiver, or whether they remain with the migrant (who is likely to now be relatively better off as a result of migrating). The second aspect is whether the poor are able to take advantage of lower-cost remittance sending methods, or whether additional policies are needed to help the poor in using lower-cost remittance options. We discuss both these questions with reference to data collected on Tongan migrants to New Zealand and Tongan remittance-receiving families. This provides a useful example given the importance of migration and remittances for small countries: the average island country with a population under 1.5 million has 17 percent of all citizens overseas (World Bank 2006b).

The first key question is whether lowering remittance costs will actually lead to an increase in remittances received in the migrant-sending country, and if so, whether the increase in remittances is less than, the same, or more than the change in costs. The cost-elasticity of remittances will depend on the motivation for sending remittances. If migrants intend for the receiving household to receive a constant amount of remittances in local currency each month, perhaps as repayment of a loan or payment for school fees, then when the cost of sending money falls, the migrant becomes better off as less is required to meet his or her obligations at home, but there is no change in remittances received in the migrant-sending country. A second scenario might be that migrants take a constant amount in foreign currency to their money transfer operator, and so any reduction in remittance fees passes one-for-one to the remittance recipient. The final possibility is that the cost-elasticity of remittances is negative, so that a reduction in remittance costs leads to more remittances being sent. The rationale for this is that the cost of remitting effectively acts as a "tax" on altruism, or on investment in the home village, raising the price of services "purchased" with the remittances and thereby leading migrants to underinvest. Lowering the cost of remittances therefore may cause migrants to more than proportionally increase the amount they remit.

To date no rigorous empirical study shows which of the above three scenarios happens in practice. Nevertheless, some suggestive evidence is found in Gibson, McKenzie, and Rohorua (2006), who ask Tongan migrants in New Zealand hypothetical questions about how their remittances would change in response to changes in remittance costs. They find that 30 percent of remitters say they would send more money if remittance costs fall, while 70 percent would keep the amount sent the same. Based on this estimate, the authors calculate that lowering the fixed cost of sending money through banks and money transfer operators from New Zealand to Tonga to levels close to that found in the most competitive world markets would result in a 28 percent increase in remittances.

However, the second step required for the increase in remittances to lower poverty in the migrant-sending country is that some of this increase in remittances be received by poor households. This will depend, first and foremost, on whether migrants are drawn from the upper or lower part of the income distribution in the sending country, as discussed in the first chapter in this book. However, in situations where at least some of the migrants are poor, it will also depend on whether policies that lower the average costs of sending remittances also reduce the costs of sending to poor households. Lack of knowledge and lack of financial access are two barriers faced by poor households in order to take advantage of lower-priced remittance methods.

In Gibson et.al (2008) we describe how these barriers prevent Tongan households from taking advantage of cheaper remittance-sending technologies. While the costs of remitting from New Zealand to Tonga are high by world standards, but there do exist at least two methods which are considerably cheaper than the most commonly used methods such as Western Union and bank transfers. These two cheaper methods are Internet-based transfer to pre-paid debit cards through iKobo.com, and the use of a second ATM card linked to the migrant's account. Not a single person in our survey had heard of the first method, and only 2 percent used the dual ATM card method, despite its costing only one-third of the more commonly used methods. Lack of knowledge is a first barrier to their use, with few migrants knowing about these methods. Financial education of the poor therefore appears necessary to enable migrants to take advantage of cheaper remittance-sending methods. However, this needs to be coupled with additional financial access in the migrant-sending country. Our analysis found ATM machines to be less geographically accessible than Western Union outlets in Tonga. Poor rural households are particularly likely to be farther away from banking and ATM facilities. Expanding financial access therefore appears to be a necessary step in ensuring the poor get to benefit from many of the policies intended to lower remittance fees. Policies which can expand financial access are summarized in World Bank (2008a).

Temporary Migration Programs Can Expand Opportunities for the Poor to Migrate

While developing countries can increase the poverty-reducing impacts of migration by lowering costs—removing self-imposed barriers and lowering the costs of getting remittances from existing migrants—ultimately to truly realize the poverty-reducing potential of migration they need to expand the opportunities for their citizens to take advantage of the large gaps in wages across countries. In particular, in a world of increasingly skill-selective immigration policies, there is a need for expanding the opportunities for poor, less-skilled individuals to participate in international migration.

Temporary worker programs are increasingly viewed as some of the few palatable ways of increasing unskilled migration.[11] Such programs are seen as relieving labor shortages in developed countries and aiding the development in developing countries, while also alleviating developed countries from the perceived costs of integrating low-skilled foreign nationals into their societies and welfare systems, and developing countries from suffering permanent losses in skills. However, to date there has been little empirical evidence as to the ability of such programs to involve the poor in practice. New data collected as part of a project to assess the development impact of a new seasonal worker program in the Pacific provide us with one glimpse into how and when seasonal worker programs will incorporate the poor in practice.

The program in question is New Zealand's Recognised Seasonal Employer (RSE) program, launched on April 30, 2007.[12] The intention of the policy is to match seasonal labor shortages in the New Zealand horticulture and viticulture industries with the excess supply of unskilled workers in some Pacific nations. One of the explicit objectives of the RSE is to "encourage economic development, regional integration and good governance within the Pacific, by allowing preferential access to workers who are citizens of eligible Pacific countries" (New Zealand Department of Labour 2007). Interested employers must first apply to become recognized seasonal employers, and then can recruit workers for a maximum of seven months per eleven-month period. In subsequent years, subject to satisfactory performance and a continuing need for labor, employers' RSE status will be extended and previous seasonal workers may return to New Zealand.

Our baseline data allow us to compare the pattern of selection of migrants in the two Pacific Island nations that supplied the most seasonal workers during the first year of the program: Vanuatu and Tonga. Prior to the program, the two countries had very different experiences with migration to New Zealand. Tonga (population 102,000) has a long history of migration to New Zealand, with approximately 22,000 Tongan-born individuals now living in New Zealand (Statistics New Zealand 2007). However, in recent years most migration to New Zealand has taken the form of either family reunification, or permanent migration through a special quota. In contrast, Vanuatu (population 215,000) has had few outlets for emigration to any country, with an estimated total migrant stock abroad of only 3,092 (World Bank 2008b). The 1,698 Ni-Vanuatu workers who had been approved to come to New Zealand under the RSE as of May 22, 2008, thus represent a huge increase in migration opportunities in Vanuatu.[13] As of the same date, 816 Tongan RSE workers had been approved, which is still a sizable increase in opportunities to work abroad, given that between 2000 and 2006, 1,365 Tongans per year on average had received approval to enter New Zealand as permanent residents.

In Tonga, employers recruited workers from a "work-ready" pool of Tongan nationals prescreened and selected by the Tongan Labour Ministry.[14] This work-ready pool was formed by preselection and screening at the district level by district and town officers, together with church and community leaders. Communities sought good, reliable people with a reason to return to Tonga, and who needed the money. There were high expectations from the sending community members to represent their village well and not to jeopardize further employment opportunities for others in the community. Figure 6.4 compares the distribution of household expenditure per person for Tongans selected for the RSE with the distribution of household expenditure per person for individuals who didn't apply. We see the majority of RSE migrants come from households with less than US$2 per day in expenditure, and that the RSE migrant households are poorer on average than households where people don't apply for the RSE. Gibson, McKenzie, and Rohorua (2008) show further that the RSE migrant workers are poorer than applicants for the program who weren't selected, and that the workers are more rural and less educated than permanent migrants going to New Zealand through the existing Pacific Access category quota system. Given opportunities for existing migration in

Figure 6.4   Seasonal Migrants Are Poorer Than Nonapplicants in Tonga

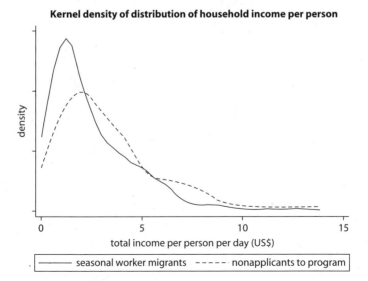

Kernel density of distribution of household income per person

Source: RSE baseline survey in Tonga.

Tonga, the seasonal worker program has thus succeeded in opening migration to poorer individuals with few existing opportunities.

In Vanuatu, two methods were used to select workers for the RSE. The first was direct selection by employers, facilitated in part by the Vanuatu Department of Labour, while the second was the use of an agent. McKenzie, Garcia-Martinez, and Winters (2008) show that the ni-Vanuatu workers coming to New Zealand are mostly male subsistence farmers with less than 10 years of schooling. These are certainly workers whose skill levels would not qualify them for emigration to New Zealand or Australia under their points systems for permanent migration, and the RSE is thus expanding opportunities for migration. Nevertheless, as Figure 6.5 shows, the ni-Vanuatu selected for the RSE are still from wealthier households on average than nonapplicants. However, it is still the case that a large share of those participating are poor: 20 percent of RSE migrants come from households with per capita income (including own production) of less than US$1 per day, and 34 percent are from households with per capita income below US$2 per day.

Thus we see that in both cases the introduction of a seasonal worker program has succeeded in opening up new opportunities for some of the poor to participate in international migration, with participation being more pro-poor in Tonga than in Vanuatu. It is still too early to ascertain

Figure 6.5   Seasonal Migrants Are Richer Than Nonapplicants in Vanuatu

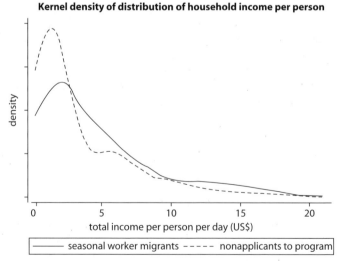

Kernel density of distribution of household income per person

Source: RSE baseline survey in Vanuatu.

the impact of the program on poverty in these two countries, but the fact that the program has already managed to incorporate many poor workers in its first year augurs well.

What then are the barriers to more of the poor participating? The first barrier is information: in both countries only 27 percent of the nonapplicants had even heard of the program. The program is in its first year, and it is to be expected that as communities gain more experience with the program, knowledge will grow. The second barrier is cost. The cost of participating includes a visa, passport, medical check, police clearance, winter clothing, internal transportation, and half of the airfare to New Zealand (the other half is paid by the employer). This cost averaged US$420 in Tonga and US$580–$690 in Vanuatu—considerable costs given income levels in the islands. The cost of a passport is US$50 in Vanuatu and US$46 in Tonga, with some in Vanuatu paying US$70 for express service. In both countries these costs are slightly above world average levels. Many workers were able to get loans for some of these costs, through employers, their church in the case of Tongans, and from a bank in the case of Vanuatu. However, it is unclear how widespread information about these loan possibilities was in advance. Other countries considering participating in seasonal worker programs could benefit from working with the private and nongovernment sectors in advance to develop such products and make potential temporary workers aware of the possibilities for financing. Policies need to both expand opportunities and lower costs to maximize the poverty-reducing potential of migration.

Conclusions

Many of the poor around the world express a desire to escape poverty through working abroad for some period of time. However, at present few of the poor actually do migrate, and developing countries do not necessarily maximize the poverty-reducing impact of the few who do. This chapter has shown that there are policies that developing countries can pursue to lower the costs and increase the opportunities for migration, and that doing so is likely to increase the participation of the poor in migration. Policies to lower the costs include lowering passport costs, removing legal barriers such as exit visas and requiring women to have their husband or father's permission before traveling, and financial education and expansion of financial access to enable poor families with migrants to receive remittances at lower cost. Given the desire of many of the poor to work abroad for a temporary period, and the fact that temporary worker programs face less political resistance in developed countries than permanent migration, there is also scope for more bilateral temporary worker programs. Early experience from the Recognised Seasonal Employer program between New Zealand and the Pacific shows that such a program does expand the opportunities for the poor to migrate, although transport costs and poor networks limit this to some extent in Vanuatu. Policy makers can potentially make such programs even more pro-poor through better information dissemination and through working with the private and nongovernmental sectors to ensure access to loans so that the poor can afford the up-front costs of participation.

Notes

1. Population Division of the Department of Economic and Social Affairs of the United Nations Secretariat, Trends in Total Migrant Stock: The 2005 Revision, http://esa.un.org/migration, April 7, 2006.

2. See, for example, Grogger and Hanson (2008), who estimate very high fixed costs of migration for some countries and that these fixed costs explain a large share of the selectivity of migration for poorer countries.

3. This is not to downplay the important role that developed countries' immigration policies have in determining the number and characteristics of migrants from developing countries. See Pritchett (2006) for discussion of policies that rich countries can pursue to enhance migration of the poor while also being politically acceptable.

4. Migrant networks can also increase the benefits of migration, such as by providing access to jobs (see Munshi 2003). We focus here on costs, since the argument is that the income and job opportunities abroad are such that poor migrants want to migrate but can't overcome the financial constraints that prevent them doing so. Any effect of migrant networks on the benefits of migration without easing financial constraints of moving will still limit the ability of the poor to migrate.

5. The paper uses historic migration networks as an instrument for the current migration network in a community. The community migration prevalence is used to measure migration networks. See the paper for details and justification of this identification strategy.

6. We convert 1997 pesos into PPP U.S. dollars using the Penn World Tables PPP exchange rate for Mexico for 1997.

7. A fuller description of the data is found in McKenzie (2007).

8. There is also sometimes a third form of cost, the "float," which is the interest earned by the bank during the time between receiving the funds from the sender and delivering them to the beneficiary (see World Bank 2006a). These costs appear minimal in the New Zealand case discussed here.

9. Western Union online data as of August 11, 2008. Exchange rate commission obtained by comparing Western Union rate of $NZ1 = TOP1.2084 to Interbank rate of $1NZ = TOP1.287 on www.xe.com/ucc [accessed August 11, 2008]. $1NZ = $US0.70.

10. There is debate in the literature as to whether more skilled migrants remit more or less (e.g. see Faini 2007). If migrants from poorer families send larger shares of their income back than migrants from richer households, it need not be the case that the smallest remittance transactions go to the poorer households.

11. See, for example, Winters (2003), GCIM (2005), Pritchett (2006).

12. See Gibson, McKenzie, and Rohorua (2008) and McKenzie, Garcia-Martinez, and Winters (2008) for detailed discussion of the baseline data from Tonga and Vanuatu, respectively.

13. Ni-Vanuatu is the term used to refer to the Melanesian people who make up the population of Vanuatu.

14. See Gibson, McKenzie, and Rohorua (2008) for greater detail on the process of recruitment and selection in the Tongan case.

References

Clemens, Michael, and Lant Pritchett. 2008. "Income per Natural: Measuring Development for People Rather Than Places." *Population and Development Review* 34(3): 395–434.

Dolfin, Sarah, and Garance Genicot. 2006. "What Do Networks Do? The Role of Networks on Migration and 'Coyote' Use." Working paper. Georgetown University, Washington, DC, March.

Espinosa, Kristin, and Douglas Massey. 1997 "Undocumented Migration and the Quantity and Quality of Social Capital." *Soziale Welt* 12: 141–62.

Faini, Riccardo. 2007. "Remittances and the Brain Drain: Do More Skilled Migrants Remit More?" *World Bank Economic Review* 21(2): 177–91.

Gibson, John, Geua Boe-Gibson, David J. McKenzie, and Halahingano Rohorua. Forthcoming. "Efficient Remittance Services for Development in the Pacific." *Asia-Pacific Development Journal.*

Gibson, John, David J. McKenzie, and Halahingano Rohorua. 2006. "How Cost Elastic Are Remittances? Evidence from Tongan Migrants in New Zealand." *Pacific Economic Bulletin* 21(1): 112–28.

———. 2008. "How Pro-Poor Is the Selection of Seasonal Migrant Workers from Tonga under New Zealand's Recognized Seasonal Employer (RSE) Program?" *Pacific Economic Bulletin* 23(3): 187–204.

Global Commission on International Migration (GCIM). 2005. "Migration in an Interconnected World: New Directions for Action." http://www.gcim.org.

Grogger, Jeffrey, and Gordon Hanson. 2008. "Income Maximization and the Selection and Sorting of Immigrants." Working Paper 13821. National Bureau of Economic Research, Cambridge, MA.

International Organization for Migration (IOM). 2005. *World Migration 2005: Costs and Benefits of International Migration*. Geneva: IOM.

McKenzie, David. 2007. "Paper Walls Are Easier to Tear Down: Passport Costs and Legal Barriers to Emigration." *World Development* 35(11): 2026–39.

McKenzie, David, Pilar Garcia-Martinez, and L. Alan Winters. 2008. "Who Is Coming from Vanuatu to New Zealand under the New Recognised Seasonal Employer (RSE) Program?" *Pacific Economic Bulletin* 23(3): 205–28.

McKenzie, David, John Gibson, and Steven Stillman. Forthcoming. "How Important Is Selection? Experimental vs. Non-Experimental Measures of the Income Gains from Migration." *Journal of the European Economic Association*.

McKenzie, David, and Hillel Rapoport. 2007. "Network Effects and the Dynamics of Migration and Inequality: Theory and Evidence from Mexico." *Journal of Development Economics* 84(1): 1–24.

Munshi, Kaivan. 2003. "Networks in the Modern Economy: Mexican Migrants in the U.S. Labor Market." *Quarterly Journal of Economics* 118(2): 549–99.

New Zealand Department of Labour. 2007. *Recognised Seasonal Employer: Interagency Understanding: Vanuatu*. Auckland: New Zealand Department of Labour and Republic of Vanuatu Ministry of Internal Affairs.

Philander, F. 2005. "Shady Deals Revealed at Home Affairs." New Era, October 10. http://allafrica.com/stories/200510100439.html.

Pritchett, Lant. 2006. *Let Their People Come: Breaking the Gridlock on Global Labor Mobility*. Washington, DC: Center for Global Development.

Sjaastad, Larry A. 1962. "The Costs and Returns of Human Migration." *Journal of Political Economy* 70(5): 80–93.

Statistics New Zealand. 2007. "Tongan People in New Zealand: 2006." Statistics New Zealand, Wellington.

Stark, Oded, and David E. Bloom. 1985. "The New Economics of Labor Migration." *American Economic Review Papers and Proceedings* 75(2): 173–78.

Stark, Oded, and David Levhari. 1982. "On Migration and Risk in LDCs." *Economic Development and Cultural Change* 31(1): 191–96.

U.S. Department of State. 2007. "2007 Country Reports on Human Rights Practices." Bureau of Democracy, Human Rights and Labor. http://www.state.gov/g/drl/rls/hrrpt/2007/index.htm.

Wehrfritz, George, and Marites Vitug. 2004. "Philippines: Workers for the World," *Newsweek International Edition*, October 4.

Winters, L. Alan. 2003. "The Temporary Movement of Workers: GATS Mode 4." In *Bridging the Differences: Analyses of Five Issues of the WTO Agenda,* 111–146. Jaipur: Consumer Unity Trust Society, September.

World Bank. 2006a. *Global Economic Prospects 2006: Economic Implications of Remittances and Migration.* Washington, DC: World Bank.

———. 2006b. *World Development Report 2007: Development and the Next Generation.* Washington, DC: World Bank.

———. 2008a. *Finance for All? Policies and Pitfalls in Expanding Access.* Washington, DC: World Bank.

———. 2008b. *Migration and Remittances Factbook 2008.* Washington, DC: World Bank.

Index